The New-Product Decision

By

Dale L. Flesher
Professor of Accountancy

Tonya K. Flesher
Associate Professor of Accountancy

and

Gerald U. Skelly
Professor and Chairman of Marketing

University of Mississippi

A study carried out on behalf of the
National Association of Accountants
New York, N.Y.
and
The Society of Management Accountants of Canada
Hamilton, Ontario, Canada

Published by

National Association of Accountants
919 Third Avenue, New York, N.Y. 10022
and

The Society of Management Accountants of Canada

154 Main St. E., Hamilton, Ontario, Canada

Kathy Williams, Editor
Mandel & Wagreich, Inc., Cover
Copyright by National Association of Accountants © 1984
Copyright in Canada by The Society of Management Accountants
of Canada © 1984
Canadian ISBN 0-920212-45-X
NAA Publication Number 84150
ISBN 0-86641-099-6

Foreword

The relative importance of new products varies among industries and among companies in the same industry as well—the latter being largely a reflection of differing organizational structure and management style. Nevertheless, it is hardly conceivable that any manufacturing enterprise could continue to prosper without being able to introduce new products now and then. More commonly, a company's product improvement and new-product development capacity is the mainstay of its continuing success. The related decision process is of critical strategic importance.

Many interrelated decisions (actions) have to be made before a product reaches the national market. This also is a process whose structure and pattern differ substantially from the decision process involving established products.

This study was undertaken to take a close look at the new-product decision process as practiced in the participating companies, to identify (describe) the decisions made in the course of this process, and to analyze the respective information requirements in light of the actual use of the information. The researchers interviewed accounting and marketing personnel at 17 companies in the United States and Canada.

Findings of interviews—company by company—are presented in Chapter 3. Individual company analyses include assessments of accounting data. The focus is on the management accounting type of information. An overall analysis of interview results can be found in Chapter 4, while Chapter 5 contains a summary followed by conclusions and recommendations. Again the focus is on the role and performance of management accountants.

This study represents part of the second phase of a continuing business decision research project sponsored jointly by the Society of Management Accountants of Canada and the National Association of Accountants. This second phase of the research project is composed of a set of fact-finding studies, designed to produce descriptive reports on a set of selected decision processes common to manufacturing firms, excluding the lower-level, highly repeti-

iii

tive, and often fully programmed decision processes such as those related to production scheduling and inventory control.

Nine decision processes were selected during the initial phase of the project. Five of the processes have been covered in previous studies: (1) distribution channels decision, (2) lease-purchase decision, (3) make-buy decision, (4) pricing decision, and (5) capital expenditure decision. The remaining three processes after the new-product decision are being covered in the ongoing studies: (1) divestment (product abandonment) decision, (2) acquisition decision, and (3) manpower planning decision.

One of the main objectives of the overall business decision project is to explore the potential for developing a management accounting system consistent with the actual decision processes and managerial uses of accounting information. This subject area will be addressed directly in the concluding phase of the project.

Guidance in the preparation of this research report was kindly and generously provided by the Project Committee:

George Bannon (Chairman)
Moravian College
Bethlehem, Pennsylvania

John H. Holzapfel
Coopers & Lybrand
Pittsburgh, Pennsylvania

Paul E. Dascher
Drexel University
Philadelphia, Pennsylvania

James W. Truitt
Martin Industries, Inc.
Florence, Alabama

Dan Armishaw
The Society of Management
   Accountants of Canada
Hamilton, Ontario, Canada

Frank L. Sbrocchi
Concordia University
St. Lambert, Quebec, Canada

The report reflects the views of the researchers and not necessarily those of the cosponsoring organizations or the Project Committee.

Stephen Landekich
Director of Research
National Association of Accountants

Table of Contents

vi

vii

The New-Product Decision

Chapter 1
Introduction and Research Methodology

Few business decisions are more complex or more important than determining how and when to introduce new products. The importance of the decision is obvious, given manufacturers' needs for a continuing stream of new-product entries and the knowledge that the failure rate is usually quite high. Some of the complexities surrounding the new-product introduction decision no doubt exist because of the aura of mystery concerning the subject.

In many companies, ideas for new products are generated, nurtured, and developed by a group of innovators. The individuals responsible often are independent from the usual lines of authority within the organization. Whereas most organizational managers are concerned only with continuity of usual operations, new-product managers are more concerned with new ideas, creativity, research and development innovations, and marketing flair.

New-product management is basically a discontinuous operation that often differs from a company's established organizational structure.[1] There are at least two reasons for the differing structure of the new-product department. First, new-product managers need to be more creative than other managers. Supposedly, this creative process does not lend itself to the company shackling managers with the chains of normal controls. Instead, these individuals, at least by tradition if not by necessity, have maintained positions of independence. Second, because new products are the lifeblood of most businesses, competitors must be kept in the dark about innovations. Thus, to promote secrecy, some degree of exemption from normal controls is required. Many managers who have desired independence probably have magnified this need for

---

[1]David S. Hopkins, *Options in New Product Organization* (New York: The Conference Board, Inc., 1974), p. 1.

1

secrecy to the point where few operational controls have applied to the department.

The success rate for new products is debatable and varies among companies. Failure rates as high as 80 to 90% have been quoted by numerous publications.[2] Alternatively, one recent empirical study estimated that only about one-third of new products fail (although several of the companies interviewed in that study had 100% failure rates over the previous five years).[3] Part of the reason for variation in percentages can be explained by differing definitions of new products. Some companies define new package sizes as new products. Others consider minor ingredient changes as new products. For instance, consider how often cleaning products have the phrase "new and improved" on their labels. Consumers probably cannot distinguish the difference between the new and the old, but the company classifies the item as a new product. Alternatively, some companies, and some authors, include only true innovations under the designation of new products. Consequently, failure rates may vary depending upon definition, but they could be much lower. We hope this study will contribute toward that improvement.

The Conference Board study published in 1980 found that management did not get unduly upset about new-product failures. Occasional failures usually were considered necessary for eventual success in the new-product market. A 100% success rate can never be assured, and any company that waits for such a guarantee probably is being too cautious and missing out on many opportunities.

In general, most companies say their ability to predict product success has improved during the past decade, and most believe their success rates will be even greater in future years.[4] The reason for this optimism is that there is a sharper pinpointing of responsibility for new products and better coordination among all units involved in the new-product introduction process. Also, companies report an improvement in their ability to predict the sale of new products.

The leading causes of new-product failure center around insufficient and poor-quality market research. Technical problems in design or production occasionally cause a new product to fail. A mistake in timing the introduction of a new product also can lead to

---

[2]For example, see Thomas A. Linehan, "Communications Boosts Chance of New Product Acceptance," *Industrial Marketing* (September 1977), p. 46.

[3]David S. Hopkins, *New Product Winners and Losers* (New York: The Conference Board, 1980).

[4]*Ibid.*

failure. Even though the failure rate for new products may be declining, there is still vast room for improvement in the new-product decision process. A company's entire future still may be dependent on a successful introduction.

Given the complexity of the management function with respect to new-product decisions, one could not generalize about this decision process based upon other types of management decisions. Consequently, a thorough study of new-product decisions became necessary so we could determine how the decision process operates. Once management accountants thoroughly understand the new-product decision process, they can use the information to design systems and provide data that will simplify the decisions. This research study was designed to help us learn through empirical analysis the structure of the typical new-product decision process.

Objectives

The objectives of this study were as follows:

1. To review the literature, both normative and empirical, in the area of new-product introductions.

2. To prepare a descriptive analysis of the decision process for new-product introductions at each of the various companies in which interviews were conducted.

3. To analyze and highlight the new-product decision process similarities among companies and to analyze the reasons therefore. Also, we wanted to note the exceptions among companies and to analyze the reasons for these differences.

4. To determine whether the results of this empirical study are comparable to the flowchart depicted in the publication, *Normative Models in Managerial Decision-Making* published by NAA and SMAC in 1975.

5. To evaluate the effectiveness of the new-product decision process.

All the above objectives are interrelated, with the overall purpose of the project being to explore the potential for developing a management accounting system that is consistent with the decision process utilized by new-product managers.

3

Contributions

The ultimate contribution from this study should be an increased fulfillment of the information needs of marketing managers—particularly new-product managers. If management accountants have a better understanding of the new-product decision process, they will be better able to supply the information needed to make such decisions. This study attempts to alleviate an oversight of long duration. Historically, accountants rarely have assumed leadership in the area of marketing costs. An earlier study published by the National Association of Accountants concluded that this condition "reflects greater concern with other functional segments of the business where organizational pressures are greater, the benefits more readily quantifiable, and the subject matter more familiar."[5] Consequently, despite all the advances that have been made in information systems in recent years, marketing managers have not fully benefited. This oversight of the needs of marketing managers is needless; management accountants can prepare reports that can be useful in the successful marketing of a product.

Accountants are not totally at fault in the matter of providing adequate information to management. Marketers themselves have taken little initiative in the quest for better accounting information. The previously mentioned NAA study of marketing costs concluded that "the major deterrent to increased use of advanced information systems for marketing has been an inability to establish communications leading to agreement as to what the needs really are."[6] In most companies, marketing executives simply fail to understand the capabilities of the accounting system. We hope this study will help open the channels of communications between management accountants and marketing managers.

This study examines what is probably the major problem area of marketing management—the introduction of a new product. The high costs of a new-product failure sometimes can destroy even a large, well-established company. Thus, it seems plausible that this area is ripe for improvements in the management information system. Ultimately, this study should contribute toward supplying the information needs of new-product managers. A fulfillment of those needs eventually should result in fewer failures among new-product entries.

---

[5]*Information for Marketing Management* (New York: National Association of Accountants, 1971), p. 77.

[6]*Ibid.*

Methodology

We accomplished our objectives by interviewing corporate product managers. We felt that face-to-face interviews would be more reliable than a mail survey. An assessment of the overall decision process should produce more reliable results as respondents to a mail survey might tend to answer the questions based on the popular literature rather than on actual practices.

The interviews were held at 17 corporations (10 in the United States and seven in Canada). At each company, we talked with the head of marketing, who may hold the title of vice president of marketing, and the new-product manager. The majority of participating companies were stock exchange listed. There is nothing magical about being listed on a stock exchange, but the companies had to be large enough so that product-line decisions are at least made regularly, if not routinely. In addition, we included a few small companies in order to analyze whether company size had any effect on the new-product introduction decision. We designed the sample selection process in such a manner that the companies studied would meet a broad spectrum of criteria. These criteria included the aforementioned differences in company size, a diversity of regional locations, and variations in product type and price (for example, the market for consumer durables might necessitate a different decision process from the market for food products).

We limited the study to the decision process at consumer products companies because the market for nonconsumer products sometimes is better defined than the market for consumer products. In fact, the customer of a nonconsumer products manufacturer may even suggest new products. Thus, the decision to introduce a new product would seem to be more difficult for a consumer products company.

Also, we limited the study to manufacturing companies. Although retailers and wholesalers have to make the same decisions with regard to product line as do manufacturers, it seems that the decision would involve less cost and uncertainty. Therefore, the sample to be studied consisted of consumer products manufacturers.

In order to keep travel costs at a minimum, the participating companies were selected from approximately three regions of the United States (Mid-South, Midwest, and Northeast) and two cities in Canada (both in Ontario).

Although we didn't use a formal questionnaire, we did use an interview tool to conduct each interview systematically. The tool, organized in a questionnaire format, is shown as Exhibit 1. See pages 8 and 9. Basically, the research involved an open discussion type of format so we could determine such things as:

1. The overall decision process,
2. Corporate and product objectives (and their importance),
3. Duties of new-product managers,
4. Organization chart,
5. The role of R & D,
6. The method of controlling new-product developments,
7. Test markets,
8. Origin of ideas,
9. Innovation responsiveness,
10. Criteria for acceptance of new products,
11. Nonfinancial objectives,
12. Techniques for regular monitoring of products, and
13. Types of accounting data needed.

Organization of Report

This research report is divided into five chapters. The first chapter consists of this introduction, including a description of the methodology. Chapter 2 is a synthesis of the literature review including a summary of the earlier NAA study plus condensations of numerous research reports from the marketing literature. It should familiarize the reader with the decision problems facing a new-product manager.

Chapter 3 consists of 17 sections, each summarizing the results of interviews at one particular company. Each section highlights the new-product decision process at the company and covers the reasons for each step in the process. Chapter 4 involves an in-depth analysis of the new-product introduction decision. Similarities among the companies interviewed are highlighted, as are atypical situations. This chapter deals with the "why" behind each aspect of the decision process.

The fifth chapter is "Summary, Conclusions, and Recommendations." In it we compare the empirical data from the previous chapters to the flowchart depicted in *Normative Models in Managerial Decision-Making.* (It *was* possible to construct a flowchart for the empirical data.) We also suggest areas where accountants can provide greater assistance to new-product managers.

6

Summary of Findings

While conducting this study, we uncovered a variety of new-product decision processes. At some companies the duties were handled at the level of division manager or president. At other companies a vice president was responsible. Even lower-level managers were the ultimate decision makers at some companies. In a few cases, the responsibility was lodged with an individual holding the title of new-product manager, but, more commonly, the responsibility for new products was only one of a manager's many duties. In a few companies, mainly in Canada, there was no one decision maker because a committee was responsible for any decisions affecting new products. Although the decision process varied widely, we were able to draw a flowchart that summarized the decision process at a majority of companies included in the study. That summary is shown in Figure 5 on page 133.

At some companies, accountants played a major role in the decision process by providing key information for the decision makers. At other companies, however, the accountants provided very little data, probably because of the lack of accounting knowledge on the part of the marketing managers who typically were responsible for new-product decisions. As indicated in the 1971 NAA study, the use of accounting data by marketing decision makers was not necessarily the fault of the accountants. Marketing managers just did not know what type of information would help them make better new-product decisions.

Some of the highlights of our findings include the following:

- Few companies have new-product policy manuals. There is a general feeling that creativity should not be stifled by predetermined policies.
- R & D is responsible for building the prototypes for all new products, but the R & D staff does not play a critical role in the decision process. R & D typically builds a product which meets the criteria established by a new-product decision maker located in the marketing department.
- There are few budget constraints on the new-product decision process. New products are considered so important that development is essential regardless of cost.
- A variety of sophisticated quantitative tools are used in the new-product decision process but at only a handful of companies.
- Most Canadian companies imitate U. S. products. Some U. S. companies also copy innovations of others.

7

EXHIBIT 1

New-Product Questionnaire

1. Describe the new-product development process from the idea stage to the time the product is either abandoned or transferred out of the new-product department.
2. What is your definition of new products?
3. Is there a new-product policy manual?
4. Are there corporate and product objectives?
5. Who originates a request or idea for a new product?
6. Who receives the request or idea for a new product?
7. Who initially evaluates the idea?
8. At what points are go/no go decisions made?
9. At any point where a go/no go decision is made, who is the decision maker (committee or individual)?
10. Are decisions made at different levels depending on size of commitment or division of the firm? (Give examples.)
11. Would expansion to a new product line require a different decision maker than would a new product in the regular line?
12. What are the duties of new-product managers?
13. Where does the new-product manager appear on the organization chart?
14. Is there a special analysis used to evaluate new products?
15. Is new-product manager a staff or line function?
16. What method is used to control new-product developments?
17. What is the role of R&D?
18. Do you use test markets, and how are they used?
19. What criteria are used to evaluate new products?
20. Are there any nonfinancial objectives for new products?
21. Are there techniques for regular monitoring of new products?
22. Are there profitability objectives?
23. Is length of payback period a factor in accepting new products?
24. Do you have a return-on-investment goal?
25. What is the importance of potential market share (% or $)?
26. What is the importance of consumer need for the new product?
27. Is product safety considered?
28. What is the importance of present manufacturing capabilities (idle capacity)?
29. Do questions of ecology and social responsibility play a role in new-product decisions? How?

EXHIBIT 1 (Continued)

New-Product Questionnaire

30. Do government regulations play a role in new-product decisions? How?

31. Do you consider product positioning (around or against competitors, target customers, etc.) when considering new-product decisions?

32. Do you scout around for new inventions?

33. Are ideas ever received from persons outside the company? What do you do about these?

34. Do you have an incentive program to reward employees for new-product suggestions?

35. Do you conduct consumer surveys regarding new-product concepts before the product actually exists?

36. How important are quantitative tools (such as CPM or life cycle models)?

37. Are calculations made of the elasticity of price and demand?

38. Is advertising used during test marketing and during introduction?

39. Are targets set for market acceptance of new products (repurchase rates, dollar volume, market share, consumer awareness rates)?

40. How long is a product monitored by the new-product division?

41. Is introductory advertising designed to result in immediate sale or to build up consumer acceptance over time?

42. What percentage of new-product ideas reach the prototype stage?

43. What percentage of new-product prototypes actually reach the test market stage?

44. What percentage of new-product ideas actually culminate in a product that is added to the company's permanent product line?

45. Are you an innovator or a wait-and-see type department?

46. What type of budget constraints do you have?

47. At what point does packaging enter the new-product decision matrix?

48. Do you perform any follow-up studies to determine why a failed product was not successful?

49. What types of new-product information do you presently receive from your accountants?

50. Is there any type of quantitative information that you would like to receive from accountants which you do not presently receive?
    (In answering the above, consider questions regarding advertising, pricing, profits by channel of distribution, profitability by container size, etc.)

51. Do you presently receive anything from accountants which you do not need or which you feel is misleading?

- Ideas for new products typically are originated by the person responsible for making new-product decisions. Salesmen occasionally play a role, but other employees and customers rarely provide ideas.
- Fewer than half the companies in the study regularly use formal test market programs.
- The primary means of evaluating new-product decisions is discounted cash flow analysis. However, this method usually is used in combination with the payback method. Estimated gross profit percentage also is used by a large number of companies.

In addition,

- Expected market share percentage is an important factor in deciding whether to introduce a new product at most companies. This factor is important, regardless of what the financial return statistics indicate, because distributors will not handle a product that has a very small market share.
- Product safety and government regulation do not limit the new-product decision process. If new-product prototypes do not meet safety and regulatory goals, the items are returned to R & D for reworking.
- Considerations of ecology and the environment play only a minor role in the decision process.
- Although given lip service at several companies, social goals play a role in the new-product decision process at very few companies.
- Idle capacity is an important consideration in the development of new products at many companies.
- Fewer than half the companies surveyed conduct any formal studies of their pricing strategies. Most simply charge a price similar to a competitor's price.
- Follow-up studies of why products failed are rarely conducted. Most managers say they would like to perform such studies if they had the available time.
- Once new products have been introduced to the national market, their progress is monitored by means of the regular product line financial statements prepared for all products. Typically there is no need for special reports to monitor new products.
- In the United States, the monitoring of new products usually is handled by a product line manager who is responsible for many products—both old and new. In Canada, the new-product decision maker normally monitors a new product for an extended period of time before turning it over to a product line manager.

• Most new-product decision makers are satisfied with the accounting data they receive. Most of the U. S. marketing managers had little criticism of accountants and could offer few recommendations for improvement. On the other hand, Canadian marketing managers seemingly had a better knowledge of accounting and were able to offer several suggestions as to how accountants could assist the new-product decision process.

• Some of the recommendations as to how accountants could assist in the new-product decision process involved the use of incremental costing, allocating advertising costs, providing more analysis of data, and being more cooperative.

Chapter 2
Review of the Literature

Many books and articles have appeared in the marketing literature on the subject of new-product introductions, especially the decision process. Almost every author has a unique idea concerning how the new-product introduction decision should be made. Given this introduction, our bibliography may seem exceedingly short to some readers, but it isn't. Initially, we scanned virtually thousands of articles for appropriateness. The publications which survived the first screening we read in detail, and we listed only the most pertinent in the bibliography. In addition, most of the references listed have appeared since the earlier study, *Normative Models in Managerial Decision-Making*, was published.

The Earlier NAA Study

The "Normative Models" study, published in 1975, defined a decision process as "any interrelated set of activities leading to a decision—a commitment to action (usually a commitment of resources)." A *decision model* was defined as a "decision process that is reasonably well-defined (outside the brain of the decision maker, e.g., in flowchart form, in mathematical notation, on paper, or in a computer memory)."[1] The earlier study was designed to describe a desirable procedure but not necessarily to describe the decision process actually used by any company.

After reviewing many articles on the subject of new products, the authors of the earlier study concluded that the new-product introduction decision was one of the most important and most complex that management had to make. The complexity of the new-product decision process is evidenced by the length of the flowchart summarizing the findings of the earlier study. That flowchart is

---

[1]Lawrence A. Gordon, Danny Miller, and Henry Mintzberg, *Normative Models in Managerial Decision-Making* (New York: National Association of Accountants, 1975), p. 1.

reproduced in Figure 1 (pages 16-19) to give readers an introduction to the various facets of the problem.

The first step in the desired system is for management to have a clear concept of the firm's mission. In other words, what are the firm's objectives? Management must know the company objectives in order to provide a frame of reference for evaluating new-product ideas. Once the corporate objectives are understood, the next step is to examine the markets and product types that promise growth opportunities. The third step involves an assessment of the limitations and restrictions management must consider. This step serves as a screening that immediately excludes those products and markets outside the company's financial capacities, its technical expertise, or the production and marketing resources available.

Step four is based on the first three steps and requires management to decide whether new products should be considered and to what extent resources can be poured into new-product development. Once it has been decided to explore new-product ideas, management must (in step five) establish an organization structure that will facilitate development. This step involves not only assigning the proper personnel to the department but also giving management an authority structure that will permit assigning the tasks that need to be performed.

Steps six, seven, and eight involve searches for new-product ideas. Some companies uncover new products by seeking out relevant technological breakthroughs. Others conduct surveys of customer wants and needs. Still others track competitors' introductions to uncover potential new-product ideas. This latter method may involve either copying competitors' products or expanding on the competitors' ideas (perhaps in terms of quality). These three basic sources of new-product ideas are used either singly or in combination and are used in step nine to generate a list of new-product ideas. Then, in step 10, the ideas are screened according to financial, volume, and goal congruence criteria established in step four.

In step 11, the decision is made whether to proceed with development on those new-product ideas which seem viable. Many ideas will be aborted at this point. Step 12 involves a survey of the opinions of potential customers in the target market. Surveys are conducted to determine whether consumers are interested in the product concept, what price they would be willing to pay, and the features they would like to have incorporated into the proposed product. Assuming there is customer interest in the product, a

14

prototype model is built (step 13). Costs and revenues then are estimated to determine whether the new product is likely to be profitable (step 14).

The next step requires management to decide whether to proceed with the new product, abandon the idea, or return the idea to engineering or R&D for redesign. Once the product has successfully passed step 15, the next steps involve the beginning of pilot production and the design of a marketing program. In step 18 the viability of the project is analyzed again. If the analysis is positive, the decision is made in step 19 to proceed with test marketing. Alternatively, if the profitability analysis is not favorable, it may be necessary to revise the production and marketing programs. It might even be preferable to terminate the project.

If the product makes it to step 20, then test marketing is conducted as a final attempt to gauge the potential success of the new item. The success of the test market is evaluated in step 21 and again a revise, abandon, or proceed decision is made. Finally, if the results of test marketing warrant it, a plan is prepared for systematically introducing the product to the entire market.

Organization of New-Product Activities

Companies have organized their new-product activities in a variety of ways. One study on the organization of the new-product department, conducted during the early 1970s by The Conference Board, Inc., was *Options in New-Product Organization.*[2] That study used a survey of corporate executives to determine the most desirable location and level for a new-product department. Questions asked included proper location in a multidivision company. For example, should new-product development be concentrated at the corporate level or decentralized or both? Also, how should functional jurisdiction for new products be assigned—as a separate department reporting to top management or a division of marketing or a division of R&D? One of the overall conclusions was that no single organizational arrangement is perfect in all situations. The differences and their importance are based on such factors as types of products manufactured, size and structure of the company, and prevailing management style and philosophy. Each of the various organizational options has its pros and cons, and tradeoffs must be evaluated closely.

---

[2]Davis S. Hopkins, *Options in New-Product Organization* (New York: The Conference Board, Inc., 1974).

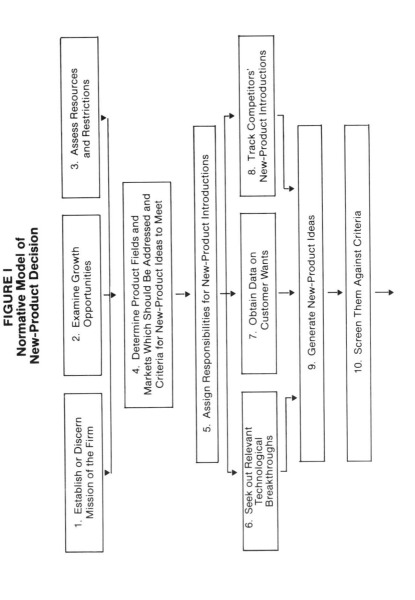

FIGURE I
Normative Model of New-Product Decision

1. Establish or Discern Mission of the Firm

2. Examine Growth Opportunities

3. Assess Resources and Restrictions

4. Determine Product Fields and Markets Which Should Be Addressed and Criteria for New-Product Ideas to Meet

5. Assign Responsibilities for New-Product Introductions

6. Seek out Relevant Technological Breakthroughs

7. Obtain Data on Customer Wants

8. Track Competitors' New-Product Introductions

9. Generate New-Product Ideas

10. Screen Them Against Criteria

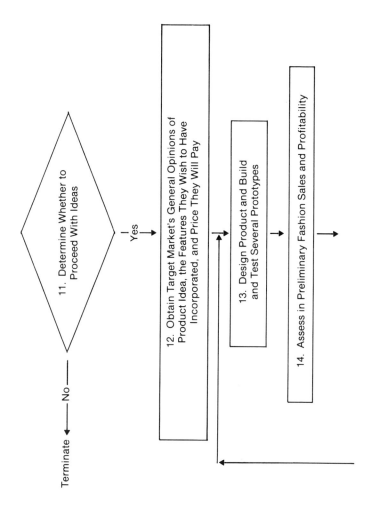

Terminate ← No

11. Determine Whether to Proceed With Ideas

Yes

12. Obtain Target Market's General Opinions of Product Idea, the Features They Wish to Have Incorporated, and Price They Will Pay

13. Design Product and Build and Test Several Prototypes

14. Assess in Preliminary Fashion Sales and Profitability

FIGURE I (Continued)

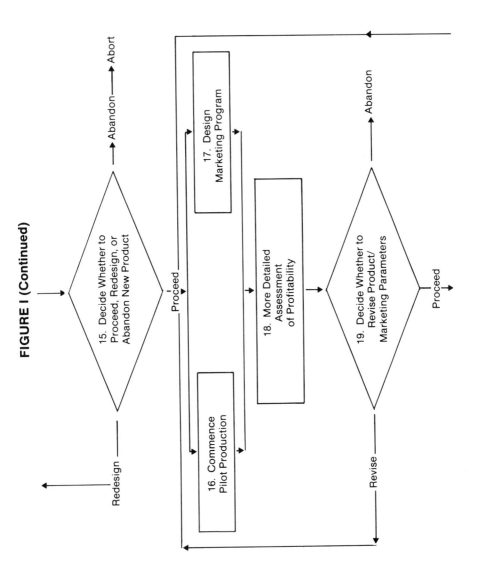

18

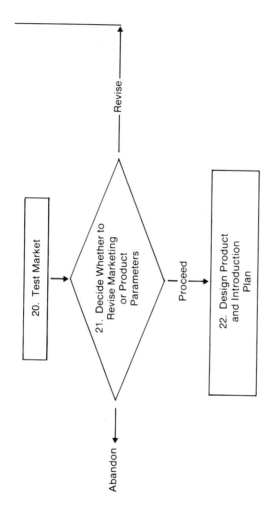

20. Test Market

21. Decide Whether to Revise Marketing or Product Parameters

Revise

Proceed

Abandon

22. Design Product and Introduction Plan

19

A small company with only one operating division does not have so much difficulty assigning a location to the new product department as does a multidivision organization. The multidivision company may assign new-product activities to the division level, the corporate level, or both. There are advantages and disadvantages to all of these options. The following sections discuss the pros and cons of locating the responsibility for new products at various locations. The Conference Board study is the source of this information unless otherwise cited.

Location at Divisional Level

Assigning new-product activities strictly to the divisional level is more acceptable when each division has separate product lines, technical skills, or market segments. Assignment to the divisional level is also preferable when new products are comparable to the existing product line and will be sold in the same markets. One of the major advantages of divisional location is that new products are more apt to be attuned to the division's manufacturing, marketing, distribution, and service capabilities. In a sense, the responsibility for new products rests closer to the ultimate manufacturer and consumer. A second advantage of locating new product activities at the divisional level is the chance for increased involvement and commitment from division personnel. When new-product ideas filter down from the corporate level, such ideas often are unwanted, whereas an idea emanating from within a division deserves (and receives) all of the support that division management can muster.

There also are disadvantages to locating the new-product activities at the division level. For example, one of the advantages was an increased commitment from division management. However, this commitment can be excessive, particularly on a new product that is destined for failure. Division management sometimes can be blind to the limitations of an in-house idea. Also, some of the factors listed next as advantages of location at the corporate level can be interpreted as limitations of divisional location.

Location at Corporate Level

Considerable merit exists for the idea of housing the new-product development function at the corporate level rather than decentralizing it, especially when the company wants to get involved in new products that do not naturally fall into any particular division's area of expertise. Also, corporate level handling is appropriate when a new product may cut across divisional product lines. Corporate level responsibility also is considered appropriate when risks are high relative to the risk-taking experience of the division.

When management feels the divisions cannot handle the responsibility, it will house new-product activities at the corporate level. This may result because of past failures or delays at the division level. Alternatively, a newly decentralized company may wish to keep the responsibility for new products at the corporate level so as not to burden division managers with an additional responsibility.

The advantages of housing at the corporate level include the concentrated coordination and control over the company innovation programs. There is also a feeling that corporate control avoids subjecting new-product decisions to narrow viewpoints and political pressures. In addition, some executives say divisional decisions more often are based on short-term profit considerations as opposed to the long-run best interests of the firm.

Maximization of return on investment also is a supposed advantage of locating new-product activities at the corporate level. With corporate coordination, resources can be allocated where the results are likely to be the most fruitful.

An additional advantage of corporate-level housing is that new-product ideas need not be tied to the types of products, technologies, and markets with which the individual divisions are familiar. In essence, corporate personnel can be dreamers whereas division staff members must be more practical. This advantage can be a disadvantage; division personnel may think the new-product ideas they are handed are too impractical to manufacture and sell.

Location at Both Levels

A number of companies try to achieve the best of both worlds by splitting new-product efforts into both corporate and division levels. Generally this dichotomy results in novel products being developed at the corporate level and product line extensions handled at the division level. One advantage of splitting responsibility is that everyone in the company, both at the corporate and division levels, is urged to be alert for new-product ideas. Such an arrangement also opens additional career paths for creative personnel by making it possible for them to transfer between divisional and corporate units.

Many managers are opposed to the division of responsibility for new products. Not only is it impossible to pinpoint those responsible for failing to come up with new products, there also is a problem with communications. There is too much opportunity for worthwhile opportunities to "fall between the cracks," according to some new-product managers. There also are problems as to how to allocate ideas between the two levels. For example, if high-budget projects are handled at the corporate level, who is to say in advance whether a specific project will require a large budget?

Obviously there is no consensus of opinion as to the proper place to house new-product activities. All organizational arrangements seem to offer numerous advantages and disadvantages. Now, to complicate the problem even more, let us examine the question of whether the responsibility for new-product decisions should be assigned to the marketing function, R&D, or somewhere else.

Marketing

What functional area should be responsible for the new product? Generally, there are three choices: (1) a marketing or sales department, (2) a technical department such as R&D or engineering, or (3) a separate new-product unit with the head reporting directly to top management.

Housing new products under the marketing function is advantageous in that new products usually will be very marketable. Most people feel that the marketing department has a better understanding of what consumers want than do personnel in other areas. Also, marketing personnel are closer to the marketplace. They know what competitors are doing and what types of complaints and desires consumers have. Another factor to consider is that the ultimate success of any new product will depend on how it is marketed. Thus, it makes sense to have marketing responsible for developing the product.

The above advantages, however, usually are voiced only by marketing executives. Other executives feel that the contributions by the marketing department are no more essential than those of a number of other functions. One criticism of total marketing involvement centers around the idea that marketers do not have a balanced perspective and often fail to appreciate nonmarketing considerations. Some executives feel that marketers can coordinate new products that are of a fairly standard type to be sold in a familiar market but marketers should not be given total responsibility when the new product involves new technology or is to be sold in an unfamiliar market. Another criticism of marketers is that they tend to settle for "me, too" products that are new to the company but not to the industry. In other words, marketers rarely come up with real innovations.

If a company decides to house the new-products activities within the marketing function, the question arises as to whether the regular product managers should be responsible for new products as well as their established brands or whether a separate staff should be assigned new-product responsibility. The executives surveyed for the Conference Board study agreed that a separate staff was preferable. Product managers simply cannot devote adequate attention to new products as current items demand daily attention.

R&D or Engineering

Historically, many manufacturers assumed that R&D was the source for all new-products ideas. This view has now changed, and marketing is out in front. In some companies that manufacture technologically innovative items, however, the R&D group is still responsible for new products. Thus, the primary advantage of housing new-product responsibility in R&D or engineering is the possibility of new inventions and the development of unique products.

Criticisms of assigning new-product responsibility to a technical department include an accusation that R&D personnel tend to be more scientifically oriented than profit oriented. Also, customer needs and requirements (including price) often are ignored. In general, executives felt that the advantages of housing new-product responsibility in a technical department were few and the disadvantages numerous. Thus, in only a minority of situations would it be appropriate to give R&D or engineering the overall responsibility for new products. In those companies where R&D has a central role, that role should be limited to the early stages of the development process.

Separate New-Product Unit

If a company is large enough to support a continuing new-product program, it might be desirable to have a separate department reporting directly to general management, not to a marketing or R&D head. This arrangement is considered preferable when new products are costly, risky, require long periods of development, and are unrelated to existing products. The primary advantage of a separate unit is that the department is dedicated to a single purpose and does not have to deal with current operations. Also, a separate new-product unit can show more objectivity than other departments and can give balanced consideration to marketing, technical innovations, and manufacturing cost.

Like the other organizational arrangements, separate unit status also has its disadvantages. One disadvantage is that a separate unit may drift away from the so-called "real world" of the factory and the marketplace. Also, other departments may be less willing to help on new products because the ultimate credit may go to the new-product department.

Task Forces, Venture Groups, and Committees

Whatever a company's new-product organizational arrangement, there are some instances when a temporary group is used to administer and control an exceptional new-product project. These temporary groups may be called task forces, venture groups, project teams, or committees. They are composed of personnel from several different departments and are placed outside the company's normal organization chart. The group usually has a direct reporting line to top management.

The use of special groups enables a company to take on projects that would be difficult to handle as a part of the regular new-product program. Also, the "perfect" team can be devised for each individual project. The use of teams has the advantage of flexibility. The group can use new approaches which are not bound by the traditional methods of introducing new products.

On the contrary, just as group members are not bound by old traditions, neither do they have the experience with new-product introductions. Another limitation is that senior management may devote too much interest to the activities of the special group. The group members subsequently lose their objectivity because of the keen interest expressed by top management.

There is general agreement that the use of special new-product groups is no substitute for an ongoing new-product program. The concept of using teams gained acceptance in firms that were carrying out one-time projects of urgency and importance under government defense or space programs. Because they were one-time projects, the companies did not think it was appropriate to channel the work through the normal new-product program. The consensus is that a team approach can make things happen once a new product has been conceived, but the team cannot necessarily be creative.

Generating New-Product Ideas

In order to come up with a few new products, ideas must be generated, screened, and market tested. A majority of new-product ideas come from a corporation's own employees, especially marketing and new-product development personnel. Some companies also use suggestion systems to generate ideas from all types of employees. Brainstorming sessions, think tanks, and other techniques also are used to bolster the creative output of personnel responsible for new products.[3]

A company's present product line is the normal place to start any search for new products. For example, modifications in a product's design or package size often can provide the basis for a so-called new product. Analysis of customer complaints also can provide ideas for new items.

Internal generation of new-product ideas is complicated somewhat by a variety of organizational obstacles such as corporate conservatism and interdepartmental rivalries. Also, true innovators are atypical employees. Consequently, these individuals may not work well within the confines of the typical organization chart and the normal nine-to-five workday. Some companies adapt to such eccentricities by permitting innovators a flexible working arrangement.

There also is a question of whether innovators should be rewarded for their ideas. Some executives argue that because innovators are paid their regular salary for creating ideas, there is no reason for additional reward when a product is successful. Also, others say that there would be less cooperation among individuals if only one person ultimately would receive a reward.

Despite these feelings, nearly 60% of the companies in one survey did have some system of special rewards.[4] The majority offered only token rewards when a patent was issued. These token awards were essentially an attempt at giving recognition rather than being an amount of money correlated with the ultimate benefits. A few companies gave sizable awards, which sometimes were given on a

---

[3]E. Patrick McGuire, *Generating New Product Ideas* (New York: The Conference Board, Inc., 1972), p. i.

[4]John T. Gerlach and Charles Anthony Wainwright, *Successful Management of New Products* (New York: Hastings House, Publishers, 1968), p. 60.

royalty basis. Another alternative used by a few companies is a contest in which organizational groups can submit ideas for consideration. Even employees' families have been encouraged to participate in some brainstorming contests.

Outside Sources of Ideas

Sources outside the company such as customers, distributors, and sales representatives, also can provide new-product ideas. Some organizations establish user panels which give feedback on both current products and new ideas, while a few companies even hire outside consultants to assist in the search for new-product ideas. Contests involving consumers also can be used (although the success of such contests is subject to question).[5]

If customers could be depended upon to generate new-product ideas, then this probably would be the least expensive method of obtaining new ideas. Thus, it might be appropriate for companies to initiate strategies which would encourage customers to submit ideas.[6] The role of customers in developing new products varies widely depending upon the industry. In some industries, such as scientific instruments, customers develop 80% of the new products. In other areas, that percentage is close to zero. Because customers are apt to develop a new product only if they can benefit financially from the idea, it is necessary for a manufacturer to establish a reward structure and make the existence of the rewards known to potential innovators.

Not all new-product ideas offered by customers will be commercially feasible. Thus, ideas should be screened carefully in the same manner as in-house ideas. Once an idea is deemed feasible, the company must obtain legal title to the concept. Even an unpatented product is protected under the trade secret law, so rights always must be obtained from the innovator.[7]

New-Product Strategy

The first consideration in new-product planning is the overall goals of a corporation. Because the universal corporate objective relates to profitability, any new-product strategy must be related to

---

[5]McGuire, *op. cit.*, p. 11.

[6]Eric von Hippel, "Get New Products from Customers," *Harvard Business Review* (March-April 1982), p. 117.

[7]*Ibid.*, p. 122.

profitability. The overall purpose of a new-product strategy is to establish goals toward which departments should be directed, taking into consideration a company's financial and manufacturing limits as well as marketing and distribution capabilities. For example, a company with idle capacity may want to limit new products to those which can utilize the unused facilities.

The target market also may be a factor in establishing a strategy. For instance, the publisher of a religious magazine may want to avoid issuing a *Playboy* type of publication (and vice versa) in order to maintain a certain image. A new-product strategy also should include such factors as whether products are to be judged on long-term maximization features or short-term considerations. For example, toy manufacturers are more concerned with short-term results, whereas manufacturers of industrial goods or large consumer products are more interested in long-term profitability.

Some companies have progressed to the extent that their new-product strategy has been established in the form of a useable model. These models help the marketing manager decide whether to continue the introduction of a particular product. One example of such a model that has received considerable attention is called NEWPROD.[8] The NEWPROD model predicts the market share for the first year after a product is introduced into the national market. This simulation model traces the number of potential buyers as they learn about the new product.

The prediction of market share is only one piece of information the new-product manager needs. Thus, NEWPROD does not solve all new-product problems. However, as the new-product decision process becomes better understood, additional models covering other stages of the development process may be possible. Another type of model has been proposed that formulates budget planning for new products.[9] The aim of that model is to develop periodically a planned number of new products for commercial development. The model is oriented toward a company's growth objectives.

All models, whether existing or potential, are based on quantitative data. Such statistics as project stage survival rate and project stage cost rate are necessary inputs into any new-product model.[10]

---

[8]Gert Assmus, "NEWPROD: The Design and Implementation of a New Product Model," *Journal of Marketing* (January 1975), pp. 16-23.

[9]Americo Albala, "Financial Planning for New Products," *Long Range Planning* (August 1977), pp. 61-69.

[10]Americo Albala, "A Model for New Product Planning," *Long Range Planning* (December 1977), p. 62.

The use of quantitative models as tools for new-product development is still in the infancy stage. Eventual reliance on such models will mean a more important role for management accountants. Alternatively, if management accountants can make the necessary data available, it could hasten the influx of useable models.

Evaluation of Product Concepts

All companies should have a formal strategy, if not a quantitative model, for evaluating new-product concepts. Reports should be prepared detailing the estimated size and trend of the market, usage rates, surveys of buyer behavior and other factors.[11] Some of this information is obtained by means of in-depth consumer surveys. Consumers are sometimes given extensive advertisements that describe the nonexistent product's qualities and are asked for their opinions of the product and how much they would be willing to pay. Companies should examine the feasibility of development and estimate the product costs. All these data should be accumulated—often at one time—for a number of product concepts.

Using this information as a base, companies should forecast the potential return on investment. Although these forecasts will be quite speculative and involve wide margins of error, they should be made. A minimum rate of return should be established, and projects not meeting the desired rate of return should be rejected or referred for further analysis. Surprisingly, there is very little in the marketing literature dealing with rate of return. Emphasis seems to be directed more toward profitability as a percentage of sales or payback period.[12] For those products passing the first formal hurdle, the next step is the development to the prototype stage, then on to a finished product.

Planning Tools

Once a company has decided to implement a development program for a new-product concept, it needs a plan for introducing the item. A number of new-product planning techniques have been developed over the years. Two of the older techniques are budgeting

---

[11]David F. Midgley, *Innovation and New Product Marketing* (New York: John Wiley & Sons, 1977), p. 222.

[12]Warren R. Stumpe, "Who Pays for New Product Development?" *Research Management* (September 1978), pp. 17-19.

and the use of Gantt charts. Gantt charts are graphic portrayals of a series of events, with horizontal lines used to represent elapsed time. Such charts have a disadvantage, however, in that they do not show the interrelationships of individual events.

More recently, PERT/CPM has received a great deal of attention as a new-product planning tool. Both PERT (Program Evaluation and Review Technique) and CPM (Critical Path Method) have been extremely effective as planning and control tools in a variety of industries. The application of CPM to new-product development even was described in a *Harvard Business Review* article as early as 1967.[13] According to that author, the first step in using CPM is to develop a marketing plan. Although the 1967 article deals with industrial products, some of the facets of that marketing plan are relevant to consumer products. For instance, one step mentioned was to prepare a manual for salespeople. Another was to conduct seminars for users. Still another step in the plan was to conduct an initial advertising campaign to create awareness of the new product and to generate inquiries. Based on the plan, a CPM diagram was drawn which involved 105 activities, 15 departments, and 22 people. Time estimates were assigned to each activity, and the critical path was determined.

Simulation models are another quantitative tool used by new-product managers in recent years. A mathematical model can be built to simulate the entire market for a product. Such factors as population statistics, economic statistics, and population characteristics such as age, education, and race can be built into simulation models. One such model is SPRINTER, which even includes behavioral phenomena and consideration of word-of-mouth communication among consumers. SPRINTER can be used to plan a test market, track early sales results, and forecast national sales levels.[14]

The planning of initial production runs is another problem facing the developers of a new product. If advertising is too effective, the company may find that demand far outstrips early production capabilities. Alternatively, if sales do not materialize as expected, excess inventories and the corollary problems of obsolescence and holding costs may contribute to unavoidable bankruptcy. Consequently, a proper balance must be maintained between supply and

---

[13]Warren Dusenbury, "CPM for New Product Introductions," *Harvard Business Review* (July-August 1967), pp. 124-139.

[14]Glen L. Urban, "SPRINTER Mod III: A Model for the Analysis of New Frequently Purchased Consumer Products," *Operations Research* (September-October 1970), pp. 805-853.

demand. Fortunately there are analytical approaches that can be applied to achieve a balance between sales and production once demand growth has been estimated and production learning curves have been developed.[15]

Life Cycle Models

Life cycle models are another tool that can be used in the introduction of a new product. The product life cycle is simply a pictorial history of a product's sales over the life of the product. It is generally agreed that the historical data will tend to produce a one-humped curve when sales are plotted as a function of time. The life cycle of various products may differ in length from a few months to hundreds of years, but the curves still can be described and defined by a second degree polynomial ($y = a + bX + cX^2$) and drawn in the shape of a parabola. The usefulness of product life cycles is changing, however, as many firms are finding that a projected life cycle model can be useful in establishing pricing and promotional strategies.

The accepted shape of the product life cycle can be compared to the dromedary; it has one hump. The product's life begins with very low sales during the market development or introduction period. Sales then accelerate quickly during the growth stage. The growth stage is followed by the maturity stage in which sales reach their peak and level off. The last stage is the decline stage in which sales fall and the product eventually goes out of production. The typical life cycle model is depicted in Figure 2 along with the trend of profits in each stage of the life cycle. As can be seen on the graph, profits usually do not occur until the growth stage, but yet reach their peak in that stage. Profits then fall during the maturity and decline stages due to the emergence of many competitors.[16]

The smooth, nearly normal curve, represented in equation form by a second degree polynomial, is not the only example of life cycle curves. One difference is between products that are accepted instantly by the buying public and those that are accepted very slowly. Those products which enjoy instant acceptance are usually "missing link" type products. In other words, these products fulfill

[15]W. J. Abernathy and N. Baloff, "A Methodology for Planning New-Product Start-Ups," *Decision Sciences* (January 1973), pp. 1-20.

[16]John E. Smallwood, "The Product Life Cycle: A Key to Strategic Marketing Planning, " *MSU Business Topics* (Winter 1973), p. 31.

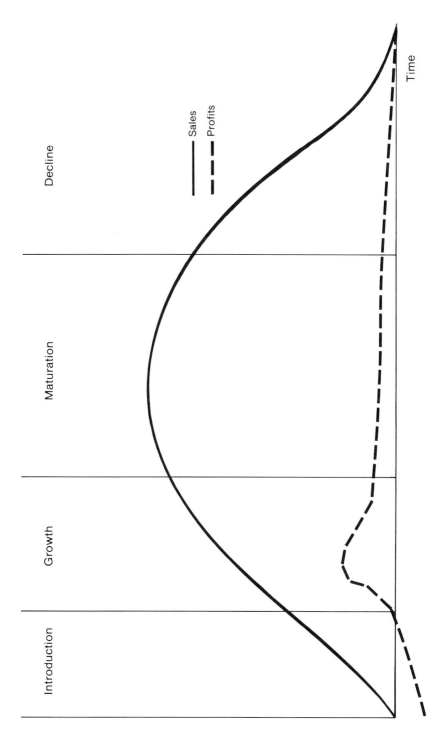

Typical Product Life Cycle

Introduction | Growth | Maturation | Decline

Sales

Profits

Time

31

a need that buyers have been attempting to satisfy. Such product innovations are typified by steep-sloped sales curves during the growth stage. An example of such a product was the black-and-white television set. Everyone was familiar with the benefits offered by radios and with the enjoyments offered by movie theaters. Adding moving pictures to the radio created a product consumers accepted easily.

Many products, though fulfilling a need, are slow to be accepted by the market. These are sometimes called high-learning products. It takes a longer period of time for buyers to learn the true benefits of these products, and, as a result, they tend to have very gently sloping sales curves during the growth stage.[17]

There is often more to the shape of a product life cycle than just the nature of the product. For instance, general business conditions within the economy can have a great effect on the shape of a life cycle. Most certainly television sets would not have enjoyed such rapid acceptance had they been introduced in 1933 rather than in the late 1940s. Legal restrictions also play a role in the shape of life cycles. Studded snow tires represent a major improvement in auto safety, but because the tires are outlawed in many states, they have not enjoyed as steep a sloping sales curve as would have occurred if there had been no restrictions on the tires. Probably the recent push toward a cleaner environment also has hurt the sales of some products. Compare the probable life cycle curve of a high-phosphate detergent introduced today with that of a similar product introduced 25 years ago. Social viewpoints also can affect the shape of the life cycle. Birth control pills, for example, do not enjoy the same acceptance in Italy as they do in the United States.

Because product life cycles can occur in several different general shapes, the predetermination of a life cycle model is not an easy process. Life cycle models probably will never be useful to some companies because the formulation of such models requires much experience upon which to base future calculations. Where a product type or class can be established so as to have small standard deviations between stage lengths (such as is true of ethical drugs), then pro forma life cycles can be established and used by new-product managers to prepare budgets, set prices, and allocate costs. Figure 3 shows the way that marketing strategies can change from one life cycle stage to the next.

Often the argument will be made that there is not enough validity to the product life cycle model to warrant using it in forecasting,

---

[17]Theodore Levitt, "Exploit the Product Life Cycle," *Harvard Business Review* (November-December 1965), p. 81.

FIGURE 3

Marketing Strategies During a Product's Life Cycle

	INTRODUCTION	GROWTH	MATURITY	DECLINE

MARKETING

	INTRODUCTION	GROWTH	MATURITY	DECLINE
CUSTOMERS	Innovative/ High Income	High Income/ Mass Market	Mass Market	Laggards/ Special
CHANNELS	Few	Many	Many	Few
APPROACH	Product	Label	Label	Specialized
ADVERTISING	Awareness	Label Superiority	Lowest Price	Psychographic
COMPETITORS	Few	Many	Many	Few

PRICING

PRICE	High	Lower	Lowest	Rising
GROSS MARGINS	High	Lower	Lowest	Low
COST REDUCTIONS	Few	Many	Slower	None
INCENTIVES	Channel	Channel/ Consumer	Consumer/ Channel	Channel

PRODUCT

CONFIGURATION	Basic	Second Generation	Segmented/ Sophisticated	Basic
QUALITY	Poor	Good	Superior	Spotty
CAPACITY	Over	Under	Optimum	Over

Adapted from: John E. Smallwood, "The Product Life Cycle: A Key to Strategic Marketing Planning," *MSU Business Topics* (Winter 1973), p. 31.

but it is still better to use it that way than to do no product planning at all. The important thing to remember about product life cycles is that they do exist. If they can be predicted accurately, such models provide a strong competitive bonus to the firm using them.

Test Marketing

Test marketing requires a major investment on the part of a company. Thus, test marketing is not just another step in the development of a new product but is undertaken only after careful consideration of an item's potential. The most compelling reason to test market a new product is risk reduction. A failure in a test market may result in a loss of $1 million or more, but this is preferable to losing tens of millions in a national failure. Moreover, a national product failure can lower the morale of the sales force and discourage investors. Consequently, test marketing, although quite costly, is sometimes preferable to a nationwide introduction.

The test marketing of a new product not only reduces risk but also permits a company to identify ways to improve profit. For example, a properly structured test market allows management to evaluate alternative forms of advertising and copy and to experiment with various price levels and types of promotions. Even alternative channels of distribution can be evaluated for effectiveness. It may be found that existing distribution systems are not set up to handle the new product adequately. In such cases, it might be preferable to sell the new product to another manufacturer who already has the necessary distribution facilities. Test marketing also permits management to learn the impact that sales of the new product will have on the existing product line. A new product might, for instance, cannibalize an existing and perhaps more profitable product. Weakness or faults in product design also can be uncovered during test marketing.[18]

Despite the many advantages of test marketing, there also are some disadvantages (besides the high cost). One disadvantage is that some types of products are not conducive to test marketing. For example, automobile manufacturers do not test market their new models because the costs of making enough cars to sell in a test market are too great—the dies and production line setup represent such high expenses. Because test marketing of autos and other

---

[18]Saul Sands, "Can Business Afford the Luxury of Test Marketing?" *University of Michigan Business Review* (March 1978), pp. 19-24.

products is not feasible, these industries must endure higher risks of failure.[19]

Time is another disadvantage of test marketing. Test marketing can take up to a year, so any competitive advantage a company might have will be eliminated. In fact, competitors usually monitor another company's test marketing program. If the test market is successful, competitors will have time to catch up and can go national at the same time as the innovator. The reason for a long test market period is to give management a feel for repurchase patterns on the new product.

Competitors may even try to disrupt a test market. For example, in one case involving a new shampoo, a competitor tripled its advertising in the test market area and sent coupons worth $1 off the $1.29 purchase price to every home in the test market city. Such tactics would make any new item perform badly. Alternatively, when competitors have felt that someone else's new product would not succeed, they have been known to buy large quantities of the new product in order to encourage a national launch of a potential failure.[20]

The high cost and questionable results of test marketing have caused the concept to lose favor with some marketers. One study found that 90% of new product failures had enjoyed successful test market results.[21] This figure has led some people to wonder how often the reverse is true—what percentage of the time are would-be successes abandoned because of poor test market results? Part of the problem can be attributed to the difficulty in finding a true test market. In the past, test marketing was conducted in a small number of carefully chosen communities, the residents of which supposedly had characteristics typical of the national population. Today, however, it is generally accepted that no single city is typical of the entire country. Because of atypicality, test marketing may or may not give a true indication of how consumers will react to a new product. Beause of these problems, computer simulation may produce more accurate results than a test market.

Many companies today do use test marketing to some degree, but there is considerable discussion regarding its advantages and disadvantages. The high costs and questionable reliability of test market results have caused some companies to place more reliance on laboratory-type test markets, computer simulation models, and

---

[19]Glen L. Urban and John R. Hauser, *Design and Marketing of New Products* (Englewood Cliffs, N.J.: Prentice-Hall, Inc., 1980), p. 419.

[20]*Ibid.*

[21]Sands, p. 20.

other stages of the product development process. In addition to keeping costs at a minimum, these latter alternatives will maintain competitive secrecy and prevent competitors from muddying up test results. Still, test markets are alive and well, at least for the present, because while other phases of the new-product development process are based on what consumers *say* they want, test marketing requires consumers to put their money on the counter— and that is the ultimate objective of every new-product introduction.

Management Commitment

There is much indication that the high level of new-product failure is more of a management problem than a technical problem. We already discussed organizational alternatives being a management problem. Other examples include a lack of top management commitment, management misunderstanding of the role of the marketplace in new-product development, and the failure to accept the risks inherent in the new-product introduction process.

A lack of enduring managerial commitment is one of the biggest problems facing new products. If new products are to succeed, they need the backing of top management or resources will be diverted to the support of established products. Unfortunately, new-product budgets are highly visible and make tempting targets during budget crunches. After all, the new-product budget can be cut (or eliminated) without any impact on the current period's revenue. Thus, in the short run, profitability will be improved by reducing spending on new-product programs although long-run efforts will be hampered by the new-product cutback. Consequently, a long-term commitment is needed for the support of any new-product program.

Surprisingly, only the long-run aspects of a new-product program usually face support problems.[22] Managers are aware of the importance of new products and are willing to initiate programs because initiating a program is relatively low in cost. However, once new-product concepts have been developed, the costs increase. At that point, managements review the costs of the introduction process and suddenly lose their commitment to the program. Introducing a new product to a market is costly, and managers often fear the risks involved. For example, in one company that prided itself

---

[22]David W. Nylen, "New Product Failures: Not Just a Marketing Problem," *Business* (September-October 1979), p. 3.

on its new-product program, 130 new-product projects had been worked on over a five-year period, but none of those projects ever reached the market.[23]

One study showed that typically a product was conceptualized, tested, refined, and verified as to potential. A product prototype then was developed and tested successfully with consumers. The next step was to prepare the manufacturing plant to produce the product. At this point, a top-management review committee invariably cancelled the project because of the high costs that would be incurred and the high risk involved. These decisions were made despite the fact that all marketing figures indicated a strong market potential. Part of the reason for cases of faltering commitment of this nature is because new-product costs are generally low at the beginning of a project and then accelerate rapidly throughout the development period. This rise in costs seems to shock managers who feel the trend will only continue unless nipped as soon as possible.

Unfortunately, managers often fail to recognize that the accelerating costs are accompanied by a decline in risk. The accumulated costs have been spent to reduce risk by market research, testing, and product development. Seemingly, this decrease in risk should be accompanied by greater commitment, but often this is not the case because managers are blinded by cost estimates and ignore the declining risk. In addition, there is a fear of public notice arising from a new-product failure. A manager who supports a product which fails in the market is going to receive a great deal of negative public attention. Alternatively, if a product is dropped before it enters the market, it will disappear without a trace. This means that one way to avoid public recognition of failure is to abandon a product before it reaches the marketplace. Thus, even a new-product manager may reduce his commitment to a project in order to avoid being labeled a failure if the new product is unsuccessful.

The role of the consumer in new-product development often is misunderstood by management at all levels. In some instances consumers are ignored. As a result, many products are developed which are technical innovations but which meet no consumer need. Alternatively, other companies are so consumer oriented that they depend totally upon consumers to suggest new-product ideas. A third alternative is to use consumers only to refine ideas that have been developed internally. This latter alternative usually produces better results as consumers are not asked to be creative but are

---

[23]*Ibid.*

asked to verbalize their thoughts about how a potential new product might solve existing problems or meet existing needs.

Another area in which management is often at fault relates to the ability to accept risk. Too often management wants to avoid all failures. There seems to be an unwillingness to recognize that failures are an essential part of any new-product program. Top management puts so much pressure on new-product managers that few new items are even market tested. New-product managers become so fearful of market failure that testing and research go on indefinitely—the product never seems ready for the market so eventually is abandoned. Instead of judging managers by their number of successes, many companies make evaluations on the basis of failure rates. Under these latter circumstances, new-product managers are going to be dissuaded from ever bringing a concept to fruition.

In summary, top management must realize that managerial requirements for new products are different from those for established products. Problem areas include organization, lack of long-term commitment, failure to utilize the marketplace properly, and an unwillingness to accept the risk inherent in new-product decisions. Indeed, all new-product failures are not marketing problems; top management often contributes to their downfall.

Problem Areas

There are numerous reasons why new products fail.[24] Some have been mentioned previously (such as organizational problems and lack of top management support). Other cases include the 11 listed below.

1. *Taking consumers at their word.* Many consumers will say yes when there is no cost involved.

2. *Trusting the test market.* The special efforts exerted in a test market sometimes can distort the results because the same efforts cannot be duplicated nationally. Other disadvantages of test markets were mentioned in a previous section.

---

[24]For example, see: Michael Paschkes, "How to Guarantee New-Product Failure," *Sales and Marketing Management* (July 12, 1976), pp. 40-42; and Urban and Hauser, *op. cit.*, pp. 577-581.

3. *Relying too much on a "good" product.* Many excellent products are failures, often because of poor timing of the introduction. Poor packaging also can doom an otherwise good product. For example, a box that is not attractive or does not open or close properly can create a serious problem.

4. *Failing to notify salespeople in advance.* Sales personnel already are occupied with the company's regular line so they really do not have time for a new product. In order for a new product to be successful, salespeople must be forewarned and motivated.

5. *Overestimating the size of a market.* The best product in the world will not be successful if no one needs it. This is one of the problems that test marketing usually will solve.

6. *Creating a product that is really not new.* Some products are really not new when compared to the offerings of competitors. Alternatively, consumers may not perceive a real difference even when one exists.

7. *Positioning a product incorrectly.* In a competitive market, a new product must be positioned so it appears to have few competitors yet satisfies consumers' preferences more specifically than any other manufacturer's offering.

8. *Failing to produce an adequate supply.* Some products meet with immediate consumer acceptance, but the company cannot meet demand. By the time products are available, consumers have forgotten about the new product and advertising has been reduced or eliminated.

9. *Misunderstanding the distribution channel structure.* There should be special functions and rewards for channel members to encourage desired actions. Again, if the product is not on the shelves, it cannot be sold.

10. *Ignoring competitive response and other environmental changes.* Initial forecasts are based on a certain state of nature. It usually is in the best interests of competitors, however, to change that state of nature by reacting in some manner to an introduction. Other environmental changes also can destroy a new product. For instance, suppose a company is about to come out with a new high-phosphate detergent at a time when one or two states ban

such products. The new laws not only will reduce the potential market, but the corresponding publicity may make consumers throughout the nation aware of the problem. This publicity could reduce the market even in those states where the product is legal.

11. *Setting prices too low to earn a profit.* The problem here is usually not with setting prices incorrectly but with estimating costs too low. Prices usually are set at what the market will bear. If the comparison of price with estimated cost indicates sufficient profit, then a decision is made to introduce the product. Sometimes it is found that costs are excessive, but it is impossible to raise prices.

Summary

On the surface, a summary of the new-product development process seems simple. A company begins by generating ideas for new products. These ideas are screened and the better ones developed into product concepts. After reference to consumer tests and other data, a decision is made whether to proceed with a prototype model and a test market. If the test market results are positive, the decision is made to produce the product on a regular basis. Although this process sounds simple, literally hundreds of decisions must be made before a product reaches the national market. One study found 105 steps in the overall process, and these involved 15 different departments within the organization.

The decision to introduce a new product is one of the most complex that management has to make. The process begins with creativity and is highly risky. To be successful with a new-product introduction, a company's personnel must be highly imaginative yet realistic. Objectivity is an important factor, but enthusiastic support is necessary, and successful development of a new product requires an interaction among marketing, R&D, engineering, production, finance, and top administration.

Chapter 3
Company Interviews

Our attempts at interviewing new-product personnel at consumer-products companies were not always productive. Some companies (including those in the Fortune 500) claimed they had no such department and no one was responsible for new products. Some companies who did have new-product departments declined to be interviewed. Most of those who did agree to be interviewed insisted upon strict anonymity. The reasons for the requests to remain anonymous were twofold. First, some managers felt that their procedures were unsophisticated, and they did not want the general public to know how unsophisticated they were (virtually every company interviewed mentioned this point). Second, they wanted to maintain the secrecy that typically underlies the new-product decision process. Managers did not want competitors to know how new products were developed.

Because of the request for anonymity, we give only the industry and general characteristics of every company. Each interview is summarized with a portrayal of the new-product decision process for that company.

Furniture Manufacturing Company

Furniture Manufacturing Company is a large furniture manufacturer headquartered in Chicago with plants located throughout the South. The company depends on a high volume of sales for each product in its line. Accordingly, it aims its products at the mass market rather than making high-priced or faddish types of furniture. The furniture industry is quite competitive, and each of the company's divisions is expected to introduce about 20 new products each year (10 at the October shows and 10 at the April shows).

The definition of new products is sufficiently broad to include new furniture shapes, new types of upholstery, differences in sewing techniques, and different sizes. The responsibility for new products rests with the merchandise manager for each product line. The merchandise manager reports to the vice president of marketing and is responsible for the profitability of the entire line. Although the merchandise managers are responsible for all products in the line, both old and new, they devote the majority of their time to new products because new products play such a major role in the profitability of furniture manufacturing. There are about 5,000 U. S. manufacturers in the industry, and because of the competitive situation a constant inflow of new products is necessary to catch the attention of distributors.

With respect to corporate objectives, the merchandise managers are familiar with only one—profitability as a percentage of sales. Objectives relating to new products are apparently unwritten. There is no new-product manual, and only tradition determines the steps to be followed in the introduction of a new product.

The New-Product Decision Process

Ideas for new products typically originate with the merchandise manager or are forwarded to that individual from the company's salesforce. Salespeople usually obtain ideas by examining products manufactured by competing companies. They also receive ideas from retail distributors and review them in the same manner as ideas from other sources. The person suggesting the idea receives no reward.

The merchandise manager visits numerous shows in an attempt to get ideas for new products. Also, he visits small furniture stores in avant-garde neighborhoods. The company typically uses San Diego, Calif., for this purpose. Once a competitor's product has been identified as having potential, that product is modified to such an extent that the resulting new-product concept cannot be considered a copy of another manufacturer's product. The company's management strongly emphasizes that it is an innovator with respect to new products.

Occasionally, the R&D department is responsible for a new-product idea, but this is rare. Ideas originated by R&D usually involve major changes in the frame or materials used in the manufacture of existing products. More often the R&D department produces the "insides" of a prototype after the merchandise manager has decided to proceed with an idea.

The merchandise manager is the sole decision maker at the point of screening new-product ideas initially. Product sketches are prepared for those ideas which the merchandise manager thinks have potential. If the sketches look good, they are sent to R&D to develop "insides" that would serve as the foundation for a product that looks like the sketches. A small production department working solely on new products is used to produce a prototype of the new product.

Although it is not a requirement, merchandise managers often will obtain the approval of their superior (vice president of marketing) before proceeding to the prototype stage if the development of the prototype is expected to be of unusually high cost. Generally, the entire cost from sketches through the prototype stage is in the neighborhood of $3,500. Costs have, however, run as high as $40,000. Because of the low cost of completing the prototype stage, most product sketches reach this stage.

The prototype product is used by management accountants to compute the estimated costs of production. This estimate is not always accurate, however, because the actual labor costs are difficult to predict. Regular production is on a production line with each laborer handling one small function. The prototypes, however, are produced in a job-shop operation and may be built by one laborer. It generally takes about one month to go from the idea stage to the completion of the prototype and the estimate of cost to produce.

Once the costs have been estimated, a markup percentage based on cost is added to determine the selling price. The next step is to determine whether that selling price falls within what the company considers a popular price range. For example, the company only will produce sofas that will retail at a price between $400 and $600. Although many sofas are sold nationally at prices above $600, the management at F Co. feels the potential sales would not warrant keeping such a product in the line. Because of this desire for high volume, some new products are abandoned after the costs have been computed.

Each division completes 16 or 17 prototypes during each semi-annual period which then are shown privately to only the company's sales staff and a handful of major distributors. These private shows are held about a month before the big April and October shows. The attendees at the private show are asked to rank the products in each line, and only the 10 best products for each line are sent to the national shows.

Essentially, the introduction at a national show means that a product has made it into the company's regular line. If show sales are minimal, however, a new product still can be abandoned before regular production begins. This process involves cancelling the few orders that were received, but is preferable to starting a production run for a product that is going to be a loser. On average, about 60% of products introduced at shows are successful and stay in the company's line for more than six months. About 10% do not meet sales expectations but are kept because they round out the company's line. About 20% are abandoned after six months. The remaining 10% are abandoned before production begins.

The go, no-go decisions in the company's process can be summarized as occurring at the following points. The abandonment percentages are averages quoted by the interviewees.

1. Prior to preparation of sketches (40% abandoned),
2. After preparation of sketches (10% of above abandoned),
3. After completion of R&D work (rarely a rejection),
4. After completion of prototype (rarely a rejection),
5. After costs are computed (10% of above abandoned),
6. After private show (40% of above abandoned),
7. After introduction at national show (10% immediately abandoned).

An analysis of the above abandonment percentages shows that the merchandise manager must come up with anywhere from 30 to 35 new-product ideas every six months in order to add seven to nine new products to the line.

Of the seven decision points listed above, the first two fall almost exclusively within the realm of the merchandise manager. The fourth point on the list is similarly the responsibility of the merchandise manager. Decisions made at all three of these points are based primarily on the aesthetics of the new product. In other words, the merchandise manager decides whether the product looks like something new and different that would be salable.

Occasionally an abandonment can occur because of the work of the R&D staff. This happens when the engineers say a concept is impossible to produce, but this is rare.

The fifth decision point is the first time a quantitative analysis enters the decision process. The management accountant's estimates are a key input into the decision process. Excessive costs result in immediate abandonment because management feels there is very little flexibility with respect to price; retail prices for every type of product must fall within a specific range. The company, however, has never conducted any studies of price elasticity. Opinions with respect to prices are based on management's gut feeling.

The sixth decision point involves a survey of salespeople and key buyers. The final decision point results in a decision based on actual sales figures.

The only profitability objective is the aforementioned return on cost. Even payback is not a factor because the company does not have to maintain inventories; products are produced only after orders have been received for at least 500 units (the minimum production run). Such factors as market share similarly are not important. The only criterion with respect to market size is whether sales for a semiannual period will reach the 500 units necessary for a production run.

Safety factors play a small role in the development of new-product concepts in that all fabrics used must be nonflammable. Government regulations also play a role in that products destined for shipment to California must be made from nonflammable foam as well as nonflammable fabric.

Assessment of Accounting Data

As mentioned previously, the major point in the decision process where quantitative data are provided is in the estimate of production costs. The only complaint with respect to these figures was that labor costs were often wrong. These errors occasionally contributed to unacceptable profit margins on products originally projected to be successful. As the price structure is inflexible, an underestimate of costs results in low profits or even losses.

Another complaint with respect to accounting was the closing date of the fiscal year. The company closes its books December 31, which means that all costs of preparing new products for the October shows are expensed prior to the time the sales of the ultimate products are made (products introduced in October generally are not shipped until at least January). Merchandise managers have complained that this procedure overstates their costs.

The managers were quite positive, however, in their attitudes toward the sales data provided by the accounting department. Sales figures are provided monthly by product and by customer. These data make subsequent abandonment decision quite objective.

With respect to budget constraints, there are none relating to new products. As long as a merchandise manager achieves his return-on-sales goal, there is no limit on the amount that can be spent on new products.

Summary

The Furniture Manufacturing Company's new-product decision process is summarized in Figure 4. Basically, the decision rests almost entirely with the merchandise manager for each product line. Essentially, the new-product responsibility is an adjunct (albeit a major one) to the merchandise manager's regular monitoring of a product line.

Although there are seven points where go, no-go decisions are made, the bulk of these are based either on the gut feeling of the merchandise manager or the opinions of salespeople. Excessive cost estimates and a shortage of initial show sales orders are the only objective factors that influence the decision process.

FIGURE 4
Furniture Manufacturing Company
New-Product Decision Process

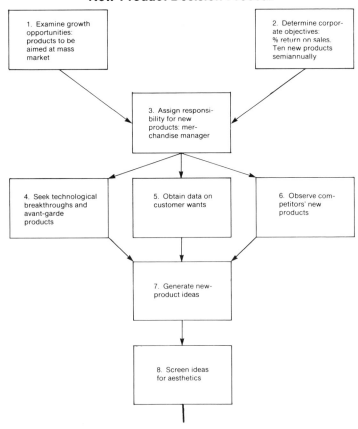

1. Examine growth opportunities: products to be aimed at mass market

2. Determine corporate objectives: % return on sales. Ten new products semiannually

3. Assign responsibility for new products: merchandise manager

4. Seek technological breakthroughs and avant-garde products

5. Obtain data on customer wants

6. Observe competitors' new products

7. Generate new-product ideas

8. Screen ideas for aesthetics

FIGURE 4 (Continued)

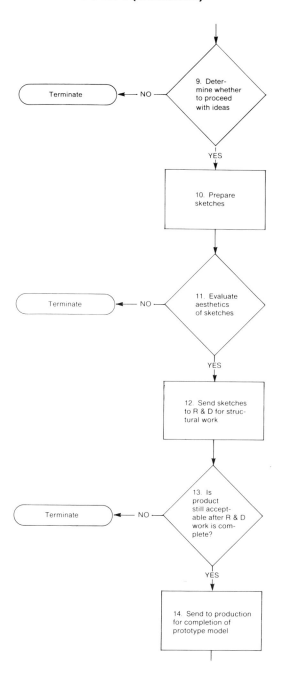

FIGURE 4 (Continued)

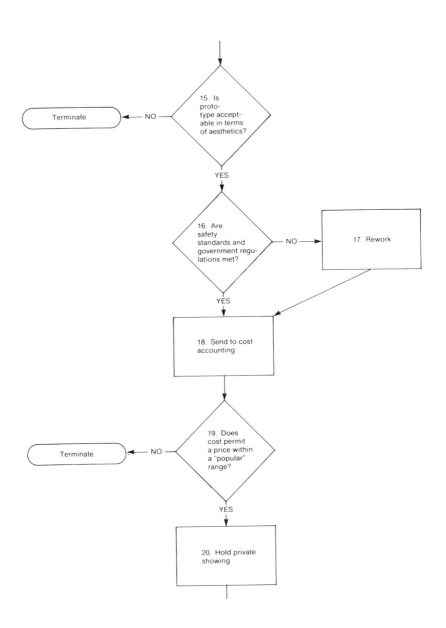

FIGURE 4 (Continued)

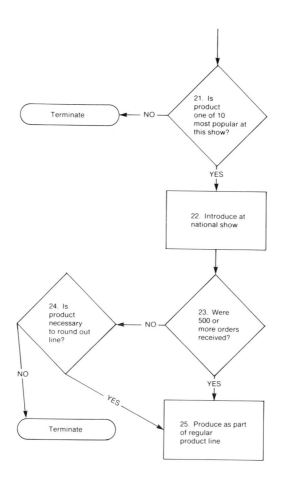

Another Furniture Company

A second furniture manufacturer was included in our sample—this one located on the East Coast. The company is New York Stock Exchange-listed and has plants throughout the Eastern Seaboard area. The story at this company was strikingly similar to that of the preceding furniture manufacturer. There was no new-product manager; all responsibility for new products rested in the hands of the marketing manager for each product line. The company recently had considered creating a position of new-product manager, but the idea was abandoned because of fear that such a move would cause communication problems. Besides, the company has been quite successful under the present arrangement.

The company defines a new product as anything new added to the product line, which almost always is some modification of a present product. The director of marketing emphasized, however, that a simple change in material can result in a product aimed at a totally different market. The company has a large product line with many variations. It advertises little, instead displaying at the High Point furniture shows (supposedly the best in the country) to introduce products to retailers.

We will not give a complete summary of the company's activities because of the similarity to the preceding company. Basically, the go, no-go decisions in the new-product decision process can be summarized as follows:

1. After the designs have been drawn (many abandonments).
2. After engineering draws up blueprints and obtains cost estimates from accounting (many abandonments).
3. After prototype is built (80% of above abandoned).
4. After introduction at national show.

The decisions to abandon at points 1 and 3 are basically subjective decisions—does the product have the necessary aesthetic qualities? The decisions at steps 2 and 4 are more objective. The cost estimates at step 2 are especially important because the company feels it has no control over selling price. For example, the company knows in advance for what price any sofa or chair will sell; thus, a pricing point must be met. Consequently, if costs are too high, the product must be abandoned. The marketing director blames the fixed price system on the competitiveness of the industry—the largest manufacturer has less than 2% of the market. All abandonment decisions are made at the level of the marketing manager for each product line.

Assessment of Accounting Data

The marketing managers and director had no criticism of the accounting data they were provided. The accountants' only input was the computation of standard costs. The company is now experimenting with the idea of putting the standard costs on the computer so the engineering department can generate cost estimates simply by feeding the data regarding materials and production processes into the computer. The accountants then will have no hands-on contact with new products in the future (unless some altogether new production process is needed). Essentially, the accountants' role will become one of keeping the standard costs up-to-date.

The marketing director admitted that the company probably was somewhat unusual in not needing return-on-investment information. Because little incremental investment is required to introduce a new product and because the selling price is fixed in advance, there is little need for any financial information other than return on sales.

Summary

Nothing indicated why the new-product organization structure and decision process were so similar between the two furniture manufacturers. The companies were located in different parts of the country. They even used different national furniture shows to introduce new items. Apparently the nature of the product (low capital investment, need for numerous new products at regular intervals, and almost perfect competition) has led to similar management strategies. Indeed, considering the variety of new-product organization structures that we found during our study, it was almost shocking to find two companies so similar.

Refrigerator Manufacturing Company

The Refrigerator Manufacturing Company (R Co.) is a wholly owned subsidiary of a New York Stock Exchange-listed corporation headquartered in New England. The corporation's operations are completely decentralized. As long as the divisions meet their return-on-investment goals, central management doesn't interfere. The president of R Co. described his company as the perfect example of decentralization. R Co. started out as a manufacturer of small refrigerators, then expanded its product line to larger models, freezers, stoves, and other large appliances. R Co.'s president (who is also a vice-president of the parent corporation) is responsible for several plants located throughout the East and Mid-South.

As with all other activities, the new-product responsibilities for R Co. are located entirely at the division level. There is, however, no new-product policy manual nor a specific department for new products. In fact, the president of the division solely is responsible for new-product activities—an assignment for which he volunteered and in which he takes pride. The president says his company is so well managed by competent people that he is able to devote considerable time to the creation of new products. His definition of new products is "new things—not new sizes."

With respect to new-product philosophy, the company admits to having a wait-and-see attitude. Few, if any, of the company's products have been real innovations. Instead, the company waits until competitors have introduced a new product, then analyzes those that seem to have potential for possible addition to the company's line. If the president of R Co. feels his company can produce a better-quality product to sell at a competitive price, prototypes are begun. In addition to improving quality, the company also makes cosmetic changes to ensure that patent infringement suits are not forthcoming. The company has never had any patent infringement problems. It introduces at least one or two new products every year in addition to new sizes in old product lines.

The New-Product Decision Process

The president obtains ideas for new products either by observing competitors' introductions at trade shows (which he attends throughout the world) or by hearing about them from the company's area sales managers. There are area sales managers in nearly every state who work with independent distributors. The area sales managers generally get their ideas directly from the distributors. Neither the distributors nor the area sales managers are rewarded for suggesting new-product ideas, but they may be able to benefit subsequently by being able to offer an expanded product line.

The guidelines which the president has set for evaluating new-product ideas include a requirement that a new product should, within 18 months after introduction, contribute sales of $.5 million per year. In addition, the product should be one that can be sold through the company's present distribution channels. Also, a product may be accepted because it fills a niche in the company's product line regardless of potential profitability.

Once the president finds a product concept that he feels has potential, his next step is to ask area sales managers for their opinions regarding the idea. Although the opinions of the sales managers are incorporated into the president's thought processes, he says he still might proceed with a project despite overwhelming opposition to an idea. In fact, some of the company's most successful products initially were rejected by the sales managers.

The next step is to turn the idea over to the engineering department along with a competitor's product to be tested and torn apart. From that point on, the director of engineering coordinates the new-product project. Generally, the engineering director is expected to come up with an addition to the product line within 18 months although it often is possible for the engineers to hand-create a working prototype within six weeks. This prototype can be used for testing and subsequent product modification.

The controller's department works closely with engineering in computing the costs of the new product. Prices are established on the basis of what competitors are charging. The gross profit margin must be at least 25% of sales or the product will be abandoned unless it somehow contributes to the sale of other products. Once a product reaches the market, sales are monitored weekly through an analysis of reports submitted by the area sales managers.

The prototype product is photographed and used to produce advertising brochures which are made available to the area sales managers. Then orders are taken. The sales organization is a more important means of introducing a new product than trade shows. A product usually is not introduced at a trade show until it has been on the market several months.

Idle capacity is not really a consideration in the selection of new products. If necessary, the company will lease nearby facilities on a short-term basis in order to get a new project underway. Budget constraints also are not an important factor although capital equipment purchases in excess of $10,000 must be approved by the parent corporation after an estimate of the time-adjusted rate of return has been computed. This procedure does not present a problem as long as the numbers indicate the new equipment is a profitable investment.

Product safety is also a factor in all new-product decisions. The company has been sued previously so it is wary of future product liability problems. Additionally, all products must meet the requirements of Underwriters Laboratories and the National Sanitation Foundation.

In summary, the go, no-go decisions in the company's process are made at the following points:

1. After initial consideration of idea,
2. After discussion with area sales managers,
3. After development of prototype,
4. After computation of costs,
5. After initial orders are taken.

The interviewees were unable to give any estimates of the abandonment percentages at each step, but they did estimate that the abandonment rate at all steps after step 2 totalled less than 5%. Such factors as safety did not affect the go, no-go decision because unsafe products are always reworked until they do meet the safety guidelines.

The decision maker at all steps is the president, and he admits to using dictatorial powers in making these decisions. He stated that he would never use such powers so dictatorially in any other type of management decision, but he feels the nature of the new-product decision process is such that gut feeling is often more important than financial facts or popular opinion. Because every product he has introduced over the past two decades has been successful, he feels he has strong support for his opinion and his actions. The president did admit that the opinion of the controller (step 4) usually was more important than that of anyone else other than himself. Eventually products are routinely abandoned whenever their sales have declined to such a level that they are no longer profitable (less than $500,000 per year for most products; products with high gross margin percentages may survive with lower sales).

Assessment of Accounting Data

The president was quite pleased with the accounting data provided to him both for purposes of making new-product decisions and for monitoring a product's success once it entered the line. Cost estimates always have been quite accurate—a factor which improves the ability to make successful go, no-go decisions.

Product sales are monitored by means of monthly reports showing sales by product for each of the last 60 months. These reports also show the gross margin for each product.

Summary

The R Co.'s new-product decision process is strictly a one-man operation. The president exercises dictatorial powers at every stage of the decision process. Essentially, the entire process reminds one of a small, closely held company rather than a multinational conglomerate.

The company's new-product philosophy is based on a wait-and-see attitude. Once a competitor has introduced something that appears to offer a substantial national market, the R Co. president begins the new-product decision process. The president's subjective opinion is more important than any objective factors in deciding whether to introduce a new item. The president admits to near 100% success. Although accounting information plays only a small role in the decision process, that information has been exceptionally accurate.

Home Products Company

Home Products Company (H Co.) is a Midwest division of a major New York Stock Exchange-listed company. Division sales are in the neighborhood of $1 billion per year. The division produces food items, toothpaste, soap products, and proprietary medicines. The company will consider producing anything that can be sold in supermarkets and drugstores. The person responsible for new products is the director of brand management. Although several brand managers report to the director, 90% of the director's activities are devoted to new-product development. The director of brand management reports to the vice president of marketing.

The company's definition of a new product is one that is new to the company and will have its own brand name. Line extensions or improvements of old products are not included. Overall corporate policies are strictly financial—there are no written guides as to the types of products the company wants to be associated with. However, because of the importance of distribution channels to a product's success, there are unwritten guidelines that limit products to those that can be marketed through drugstore and grocery channels. The division has a goal of introducing at least one new product each year to the national market.

The New-Product Decision Process

The new-product policy manual prescribes the route to be

followed in the new-product decision process. The first step involves an analysis of consumer behavior. For example, the company has conducted studies of consumers' bathing habits. Surveyors have learned every aspect of consumers' likes and dislikes about taking a bath. Once all the information about a particular consumer habit is known, the brand managers and new-product employees analyze the findings to see if they can discover a consumer need that is not being met fully by present products. The company emphasizes consumer needs, not products. The director of brand management contrasted his company's objective with that of many other companies. H Co. does not try to find new products; it tries to find consumer needs.

Once an unmet need has been discovered, the idea is turned over to R&D with instructions to develop a product that will meet the defined needs of consumers. About 60% of the time R&D is successful in producing the item requested.

The prototypes of the new product then are used to conduct blind tests in which consumers are asked whether the new product or a competitor's product is better. At least two-thirds of the prototypes win the blind comparison tests and are slated for test marketing.

The company uses two types of test marketing programs. One type is a regional test market in which about 4% of American families are included in the test market area. When secrecy is considered important, however, a laboratory test market is used instead of a regional market. The laboratory test market used by H Co. is conducted by Yankelovich Associates. Pricing alternatives are considered a part of the test marketing program. About half the products test marketed are successful and are introduced to the national market. The product is then turned over to a brand manager for regular monitoring.

Following the completion of a successful test market, the accountant enters the picture with calculations of costs, payback period, and return on investment. Of course these estimates are dependent on the volume projections resulting from the test market results. The percentage of market share is not important to the company as long as the dollar volume is adequate. If market share is too small (for example, 1%), however, a product would have to be abandoned because of lack of interest in the distribution channels.

Occasionally the director of brand management will receive an idea for a new product from a consumer, company salesperson, or other employee. Also, there is a new-product staff which keeps up with the competitors' activities. In addition, R&D does some "blue sky" research and occasionally invents a new product of its own. If the director likes these ideas, he will initiate the aforementioned behavioral studies to determine whether the new ideas are indeed viable. The company provides no incentive nor gives any reward for products conceived by employees.

Additional factors that have to be considered before a product is placed on the market are social responsibility and federal regulations. These factors usually have to be considered prior to the time the product concept is sent to the R&D department. The social responsibility aspects usually are important only with respect to proprietary medicines. The company feels that there are many successful products being marketed legally by competitors that are not totally safe for consumer use. Thus, the company will not compete in these areas despite having the necessary expertise and facilities.

Federal regulations also play a role in selecting the ingredients that can go into many products. For example, there is a limitation prescribed by the Food and Drug Administration as to the maximum level of certain ingredients that can be included in any product.

The go, no-go decisions in the company's new-product decision process occur at the points listed below:

1. After a behavioral study has been conducted,
2. After consideration of federal regulations and the company's social responsibility,
3. After development by R&D,
4. After blind comparison tests have been conducted,
5. After test marketing,
6. After completion of return-on-investment calculations.

The above decisions are made jointly by the director of brand management and the vice president of marketing. The director emphasized that the decision is very objective after the first three points made above. For example, the blind tests must show that at least 60% of consumers prefer the new product. Similarly, if return-on-investment estimates are not high enough to meet company goals, then a product is abandoned without hesitation. With the large investments involved in introducing new products, the director felt there was no room for "gut feelings" in the decision process.

As for success rates, the director stated that for every five ideas turned over to R&D, about three prototypes resulted. Two of these usually pass the blind comparison tests. Only one generally reaches the national market. There is some difficulty in determining whether this last abandonment decision occurs after the test market or after the return-on-investment calculations as the two are interrelated. Essentially, the test market program is designed to provide data for use in the financial calculations.

Assessment of Accounting Data

The accounting department is responsible for estimating the costs of production and for computing the return on investment and payback period. This is the only accounting information provided. Even sales of the new products is not provided. Instead, the marketing group prefers independent estimates of retail sales over the dollar volume of company shipments.

The director had no criticism of the accounting department. Cost allocations have seemed reasonable, and estimates have been accurate enough for decision purposes.

Summary

The Home Products Company's new-product decision process is spelled out in the company's new-product policy manual and is quite objective. The responsibility for new products is housed with the top marketing person at a billion-dollar (sales) division.

Although the work of accountants is minimal, much of the testing is for the purpose of generating data to be used by accountants in computing investment returns. The director summarized his feelings that management's objectivity can be traced to the fact that products are not developed until after needs are recognized. Many of the companies in this survey developed a product and then tried to sell it. H Co. first recognized a consumer need so knew what would sell before the product existed. Consequently, there was no "love affair" with a "pet product." Therefore, management based its decisions on numbers rather than instincts.

Another Home Products Company

Another company in our sample produced home cleaning supplies and food products. This company is similar to the preceding company in that it would consider any product that could be marketed through drugstores and supermarkets. Like the preceding company, it is located in the Midwest (but several hundred miles from the other company). Because of the similarity of the new-product decision process between these two companies, we will not give a complete summary of this second company except where procedures differ from those of the preceding company.

Even the organization of the new-product responsibility was similar except that the head of the new-product staff was called the new-product manager. He reported directly to the vice president of marketing. This company, too, was a large division of a decentralized New York Stock Exchange-listed firm.

Essentially there was no difference between this company's new-product decision process and that of the previous firm. Basically, anything that was said about the preceding company would apply to the one now being discussed. Even the assessment of accounting data was similar between the two companies. This firm, however, relied only on regional test marketing as opposed to laboratory test marketing.

These two unrelated home products companies had very similar new-product organizations and decision processes. The reasons for the similarity are unknown, but there were several high-ranking marketing people at each company who had received their early experience at a third company—one which is considered the leader in this field. Thus, it is possible that the similarity of organization may be traced either to the practices of the industry leader or to the mobility among managers in the field.

Personal Care Products Company

Personal Care Products Company (P Co.) is a major division of a New York Stock Exchange-listed company and is located in New England. Products manufactured include soaps, shampoos, and other personal care products. The person responsible for new products holds the title of director of new products and reports to the director of marketing. These two individuals essentially make a joint decision during the early stages of the new-product decision process where a go, no-go decision is made. At later stages, other individuals are added to the decision-making process so that the decisions are always group decisions and not individual decisions.

Every division of the company has its own written mission statement, area of responsibility, and objectives. There are no written guidelines with respect to the new-product development process, but the company does have specific forms which must be filled out at every stage of the development process. In addition, there are specific unwritten guidelines which are followed. The only corporate-level guidelines that affect the new-product decision would be expected payback period and return on investment.

The company's definition of a new product is anything that will meet currently unmet consumer needs. The company is quite marketing oriented, so all new products have to be something recognized by consumers as an important need. Such a product will, therefore, be more easily marketed than would a product not already identified as necessary.

The New-Product Decision Process

The new-product development process begins with the recognition of a new-product idea, which often is accomplished by conducting interviews with consumers and asking what needs are currently unmet or not being met satisfactorally. Ideas also come from the R&D department which sometimes develops a new product and turns it over to the director of new products to determine the market potential. Other employees in the company are encouraged to submit ideas for new products, and an incentive program exists to reward employees outside marketing and R&D who submit ideas which ultimately become new products. In addition to developing its own ideas, the company monitors the success of new products introduced by competitors.

The initial go, no-go decision is made while an idea is still in a rough stage. The criterion for proceeding is whether the product idea falls within the division's mission statement. If not, the idea is either abandoned or passed on to the director of new products at another division. Product ideas which *do* fall within the division's mission statement are firmed up by discussing them with consumers. The firmed-up idea is then formally evaluated by the new-products group (which, at this point, consists of the director of marketing, director of new products and two assistants from the new-products department). If the group feels a new-product idea is potentially profitable, the idea is turned over to R&D for prototype development.

Also important in making the decision to develop a prototype are such factors as government regulation, ecology, and other social concerns. The company is very image conscious and feels that any consumer products company sometimes must forego profitable opportunities in order to maintain a "clean" image.

Once the company has developed a prototype, it asks consumers to evaluate the finished product. At this time, the company evaluates the quality of the product along with most desirable packages, pricing potentials, and the preferability of various distribution channels. At the same time the marketing research studies are being conducted, the engineering department, legal department, and sales manager get involved. Engineering estimates manufacturing time and cost. The sales manager develops a marketing strategy which includes types of advertising media to be used, advertising dollars to be spent, and distribution channels to be used. The legal department determines whether the brand name selected is legal for the company to use. At the same time all this is happening, the director of new products selects a test market city (or cities). Salespeople in the test market area usually have to be trained and encouraged prior to the introduction.

The test market is conducted over a period of at least six months. This extended period of time is necessary in order to calculate repurchase rates. Once the test market results are known, the accounting department feeds the results into a model to determine how successful the product will be if introduced nationally. In addition to the test market results, other inputs to the model to determine payback and return on investment include manufacturing costs, selling costs (including advertising and distribution channel alternatives), and pricing alternatives. The expected life cycle of the product also is considered, and there is a careful matching of all marketing costs to the revenues generated.

There are three basic outputs from the financial analysis process: payback period, return on investment, and market share (in percent). A new product must pass all three tests before it is introduced nationally. These criteria are guidelines which have been established at the corporate level. The reason for having a market-share criterion is because a product that does not meet at least a minimum threshold of market share will lose the interest of members of distribution channels. Thus, a minimum market share is required to ensure that the channels will continue to market the product.

If a product fails the financial tests, the company must determine why. The company already has invested a great deal of money in the new product so it is imperative to try to determine why a product with so much potential proved unsuccessful. Again, the company accomplishes this objective by conducting marketing research studies. If the surveys pinpoint a reason for failure, a decision is made whether the product can be revamped to alleviate the problem. If so, a new test market area is selected and the process begins again. This latter decision, however, has some subjective elements to it. Because competitors have no doubt been monitoring the test market themselves, they already may have developed a better product and thus already met those previously unmet consumer needs. Thus, the entire product idea must be re-evaluated after a failure in a test market.

A new product that meets each of the three financial tests is introduced nationally. The company is careful to try to replicate the steps taken to introduce the product in the test market area.

We also must mention the lack of importance of idle capacity in the new-product decision process. We found idle capacity to be of no significance whatsoever, and no new product had ever been introduced for purposes of filling idle capacity. The consumer need for a new product is the company's only consideration. It should be noted, however, that the existence of idle capacity could influence the financial analysis and the success of the product.

The go, no-go decisions in P Co.'s new-product decision process occur at the following points:

1. After idea has been determined,
2. After evaluation of product with regard to the division's mission statement,
3. After idea has been firmed up by obtaining consumer input,
4. After consideration of government regulations and ecological and social concerns,
5. After development of prototype product,
6. After market research studies of prototype,
7. After computation of payback, rate-of-return, and expected market share (all of which are based on quantitative data resulting from test marketing and engineering studies),
8. After determination of reason for test market failure.

All of the above decisions are made on a group basis. Initially, only marketing people are involved in the group, but at step 5 an R&D person is added to the group. An engineer and an accountant are added to the group at step 6.

For secrecy reasons, the company was unwilling to provide abandonment rates, although management did admit to many abandonments—particularly at the first six points in the decision process.

Assessment of Accounting Data

The accounting department at P Co. probably plays a more important role in the new-product decision process than at any other company in our survey. The company describes its accountants as being at the hub of the entire decision process. Essentially the accounting department obtains inputs from engineers, manufacturing supervisors, sales managers, advertising agencies, private test market tracking (audit) firms, and marketing researchers. These inputs are fed into a sophisticated computer model, and results are provided in the form of payback period, return-on-investment, and expected market share—all calculated numerous times based on a variety of assumptions. The degree of risk is built into the analysis process as higher rates of return are required for those projects requiring higher initial investments. The various assumptions normally considered by the model include alternative pricing strategies, advertising media, distribution channels, and packaging schemes. Such factors as learning curves and the fixed, variable, or semi-fixed nature of costs are built into the planning model.

The same data that are used to make the new-product introduction decision are used to prepare the budget for the coming year. Because the test market results have been used to determine the most advantageous course of action, those same data are used to prepare a budget. Thus, there is follow-up on every decision to introduce a new product. The same data used to make the decision are used in the control process.

In summary, the management decision-making process is highly integrated with the managerial accounting system. The same data used to make a decision are used to prepare a budget against which actual results are compared. Accounting does indeed serve as the hub of the new-product decision process.

Summary

The new-product decision process at P Co. is quite sophisticated. The necessity for investing large amounts of capital before a product is ever introduced makes it mandatory for the company to plan every phase of the development process carefully. The company relies heavily on marketing research to come up with viable new products.

The accounting department also plays a major role once the new product reaches the test market stage. Because so many objective data are generated during the test market stage, the accountant is needed to quantify the various interrelationships. The company even has a variety of special forms that are prepared and sent to accounting at each stage of the new-product development process.

Although management was unwilling or unable to discuss the success ratio of the new-product department, it can be presumed that the system used is more than adequate as the company is the industry leader in most fields in which it participates and both sales and earnings have grown at least 15% per year for the past decade. Managers emphasize, however, that their efforts are directed toward the long view rather than short-term results. Consequently, heavy investment in new-product development is essential to the company's success and will continue.

Pet Care Products

Pet Care Products, located in the upper Midwest, is a privately owned company with sales in excess of $70 million per year. The company has grown sixfold over the past five years, primarily as a result of the internal development of several successful new products. The vice president of marketing is responsible for all new products. He was hired five years ago and assigned the task of expanding the company's product line significantly. The vice president formerly worked as the new-product manager at a Fortune 500 consumer products company. Pet Care deals primarily in pet care products marketed through grocery and pet store channels.

Much of the decision process affecting new products is parallel to that at the home care products companies discussed earlier. For example, the company is oriented toward solving the needs which have been noted by consumers. In other words, a new product is not developed until after a ready market has been identified. The company has a written new-product policy manual which was developed by the marketing research firm of Booz, Allen, and Hamilton, Inc. Pet Care differs from the aforementioned home care products manufacturers in that it is privately held and subject to the whims of a president who has no stockholders to whom he is responsible. Consequently, the president sometimes has "gut feelings" and will overrule objective data and ignore the steps outlined in the new-product policy manual.

The New-Product Decision Process

The new-product development process begins with behavior and attitude studies to determine how consumers feel about a particular pet care product area. For example, a tester might ask, "Do you ever reward your cat for doing tricks? Why or why not? How?" Based on these interviews, the company develops product concepts. Concept statements are prepared, which look like newspaper advertisements, and these advertisements for nonexistent products are shown to a consumer panel. The consumers are asked whether they would be willing to buy the product and, if so, how much they would be willing to pay.

If the consumer panel finds a product concept acceptable, then the Pet Care R&D staff tries to develop such a product or conducts a search to see if such a product already exists. If the product does exist Pet Care will try to buy the rights to it. In many cases, the company's management knows that the product already exists before it conducts the attitude studies. Management feels that marketing is such an important factor in the industry, however, that a small competitor with an outstanding product might fail because of an inadequate marketing program. Thus, Pet Care could take someone else's failure and make a success of the item. In addition, as Pet Care is a small company, it sometimes can be successful with products that large companies in the industry would abandon for lack of volume. For example, the vice president told us Ralston Purina probably would abandon a new product that promised only $7 million a year in sales for lack of volume. For Pet Care, that same volume would be a major addition to the company's product line.

Once a new product has been developed or acquired, the company gives samples—in unmarked packages—to a panel of consumers. If over 65% of the panel members feel the new product is superior to anything presently on the market, then a decision is made to proceed to the test market stage.

Before starting the test market, the company estimates the costs of manufacturing and selling the product. Four different test market areas are used simultaneously. Test market prices are set at two different levels in order to measure the price elasticity of the product, and success at either of the price levels will mean a profitable product. Success in a test market is measured by a product that gains at least 8.4% of the market share. The vice president has estimated that this level of market share is necessary to keep the members of distribution channels interested in the product. A product that achieves an 8.4% or greater market share in one or more of the test market areas is introduced nationally.

The company is not limited by any government regulations, and product safety is generally not a factor. Prior to test marketing, however, company lawyers examine the product with respect to such matters as trademark and patent infringement.

Products that fail to make the test market cutoff are evaluated to determine the reasons for failure. Occasionally, a failure is caused by a mistake in marketing or a minor product deficiency. Sometimes such problems can be alleviated, and the product then re-enters the test market phase.

The go, no-go decisions can be summarized as occurring at the following points:

1. After evaluation of concepts by a consumer panel,

2. After development of the prototype,
3. After a home placement test,
4. After test marketing,
5. After re-evaluation of test market failures.

The vice president of marketing is responsible for making the go, no-go decision at each of the above points. All decisions are made essentially on the basis of objective data. It could be said that point 2 above is not exactly objective, but a product usually is not rejected at that point unless the prototype fails to meet the criteria established in the product concept statement. The last decision point—after the evaluation of test market failures—generally is based on subjective data.

The decision process outlined above is the one shown in the new-product policy manual and generally is followed by the company. The president, however, likes to keep a watchful eye on all new-product activities and reserves the right to reverse any decision made by the vice president. The president has never forced the abandonment of a new product which the vice president's statistics indicated would be successful, but he occasionally has required a product to be introduced even though the objective data indicated a probable failure. The objective data have usually proven correct on these occasions. The president, however, has not let these failures cause him to back down when making subsequent decisions. He says that there is still room for gut feelings to play a role in the new-product decision process.

Pet Care's management were unwilling or unable to give abandonment rates at each stage of the development process. The vice president did state that all products which met the test market criteria were generally successful when introduced nationally. The company's only failures have been products that failed some objective criteria but were introduced anyway because they were pet projects of the president.

Assessment of Accounting Data

Unlike the situation at some of the companies interviewed, the accountants at Pet Care provided cost figures and return-on-investment data prior to the time of test marketing. They estimated volume at the minimum acceptable level and deemed the product acceptable if that level was met. The accountants actually do not hold a decision-making role, however, although the vice president does rely on accounting data when setting prices.

The vice president is not hampered by any budgeting constraints because new products are considered to be so important that development must proceed at almost any cost. Presumably, the president could step in at any time and limit funds for a particular project, but this has never happened.

Summary

The new-product decision process at Pet Care is probably good evidence of how the risks of innovation can be reduced through a well-conceived and professionally managed program of new-product development. The corporation has a well-organized system, and as long as that system has been followed, the company has been successful. When management has elected to deviate from that system, however, the results have not always been acceptable.

The company's system for developing new products can be compared to the systems at the home care products firms discussed earlier in that consumer need plays a major role at the beginning of the process. The product itself is not even invented until after the market has been identified. Pet Care and the home care products companies also are similar in that each makes a large investment in inventories before introducing the product. Similarly, advertising plays a major role in the marketing of both types of of products.

Sporting Goods Manufacturing Company

Sporting Goods Manufacturing Company (S Co.) is a small producer of a variety of items marketed primarily through sporting goods stores and specialty departments of department and discount stores. S Co. formerly was a division of a Fortune 500 company but was sold several years ago and is now independent and listed over-the-counter. The company, located in the Midwest, is among the industry leaders in several of its product fields.

The individual ultimately responsible for the development of new products holds the title of vice president of marketing. There is no new-product department per se. Instead, the vice president of marketing puts together a group to develop any new-product idea that has potential. The definition of a new product is quite broad and includes refinements and improvements of existing products. One example the company gave of a major new-product introduction from a few years ago was the development of yellow tennis balls to compete with the previous all-white varieties. This color change was described as one of the most significant new products ever to hit the industry.

The sporting goods industry is unique in that trade association rules limit the nature of new products that can be introduced. For example, U.S. Golf Association rules limit the size of golf clubs and the texture of the balls. Essentially, these rules are designed so that manufacturers cannot create products that play too well. Because of the limitations on product size and shape, companies in the industry rely heavily on chemistry and engineering to create products that play better. Advertising of new products also is quite important because consumers must believe any improvements.

The company does not have any written objectives for new products although it is understood that any new items should be marketable through the company's normal distribution channels. Also, the company does not want to get involved with any fad items. Only products that are apt to make a lasting contribution to the company's success will be considered. High volume also is one of the unwritten rules covering new products. The company aims its products at the mass market, so all new products must be something that the average weekend player, not just the pro players, would use.

The vice president of marketing also has some nonfinancial objectives for new products. The company wants to maintain a creative, avant-garde image. Thus, it occasionally will market a low-volume product to create a certain image. Also, products of smaller than normal size that are made for children are marketed regardless of profitability. Management hopes that children who begin with the company's downsized equipment will graduate to the adult equipment.

Overall corporate objectives affecting new products are limited to return-on-investment goals and expected payback. Usually a new product must have a payback of two years or less; eight months is typical.

The New-Product Decision Process

The company obtains ideas for new products from a variety of sources. The vice president of marketing receives suggestion letters from the public, salespeople, suppliers of raw materials, and professional players in a particular sport. Many people—usually retirees—bring prototypes to the company. The vice president said that he is offered at least 10 new putters every year from retiree inventors. All of these prototypes would be considered as true innovations as they look nothing like the standard putter. The company tests the prototypes but usually rejects them because they would not help all players as much as they did the inventor. Occasionally the company does buy an idea from one of these part-time inventors or from a smaller sporting goods manufacturer which has developed a new product. The company tends to be an innovator primarily, but occasionally a competitor's new product will be copied (with cosmetic changes). Patents are considered of little or no value. Once an idea is found acceptable, it is sent to the engineering department for prototype development or refinement. The engineering department also plays an important role in the idea development stage as a great deal of ongoing R&D work is performed on the company's present product line. The R&D group is continually experimenting with variations in raw materials in an attempt to come up with equipment that will play better than the company's current product offerings.

One of the key factors in making the decision to proceed with a new-product idea is the existence of idle capacity. Most of the company's products are seasonal, so many manufacturing facilities are idle for months at a time. Consequently, one objective of the new-product decision process is to come up with products which can be manufactured with present facilities during the off-months.

Once a prototype has been developed and laboratory tested, the company's advertising agency becomes involved. Consumers have seen so many ads for quack items that promise to improve their game that such ads now often lack believability. Therefore, the agency is involved at an early stage so it can assess the nature of the advertising campaign that might support a new entry into the company's product line. The fact that a new product is superior to existing equipment is not enough; consumers must view that superiority as being able to help their game.

If the advertising people feel they can come up with a successful campaign, the company asks its accountants to determine production costs and estimate return on investment and payback. Budget preparation for the new product relies on the product life cycle to a considerable extent. The company tries to achieve extremely high profit margins during the introductory and growth stages. Lower margins are acceptable once a number of competitors have entered the market.

Once costs have been computed, selling prices are established and the product is introduced. The company does not use test markets in the true sense of the concept, but for products that generally are used only during warm months (such as golf equipment), the company will make the introduction during the winter months in a warm climate state such as Florida or Arizona. If the product is not successful in this test market, there is the opportunity of killing the product before introducing it nationally. Sometimes the products are test marketed without a brand name so that if the Florida or Arizona consumers do not like the new product, the company's image will not be tarnished. The test market results are monitored via weekly reports from company salespeople.

One reason the company often elects not to use a test market is because of its desire to get an item on the market before there is a rule against it. If trade association rules are silent on the acceptability of a new product, management wants to get as many products into consumer hands as possible before a ruling is issued. There is a general belief that if thousands of consumers are already using a product, rulemakers will not want to risk offending early buyers. Therefore, if the rulemakers are kept in the dark about the existence of a new product, there is a greater chance the product will be ruled acceptable.

The go, no-go decisions can be summarized as occurring at the following points:

1. After consideration of the idea,
2. After evaluation of prototype,
3. After evaluation by advertising agency personnel,
4. After computation of financial data,
5. After introductory marketing in limited areas.

All these decisions are made by the vice president of marketing, who considers hundreds of ideas each year. Approximately 50 result in refined prototypes. Many prototypes are never completed because of the importance of safety factors—every product has to be at least as safe as similar products that are already on the market. Only about 10 ultimately are introduced. The rejection of prototypes usually results from either a lack of opportunity for a strong advertising campaign (step 3) or a failure to meet financial guidelines (step 4). Abandonment after limited marketing in a warm climate occurs very infrequently. As mentioned previously, the vice president of marketing sometimes will elect to market a product despite unfavorable financial statistics if the product can be expected to meet some of the company's nonfinancial objectives.

Assessment of Accounting Data

Accountants play an important role in the new-product decision process at S Co. The vice president of marketing had no criticism of the accounting data he had received over the years. Essentially, the management accountants' role consisted of calculating costs to manufacture, computing return on investment, and preparing budgets. All these activities were based on inputs received from engineers, advertising agents, and the marketing staff.

One unique aspect was the basing of budget figures on the position of a product in its life cycle. There really were no budget constraints associated with the new-product development process. As long as the vice president of marketing was meeting his return-on-investment goals, there was no limit as to the amount he could spend on new ideas.

The vice president of marketing also said that accounting data are quite accurate and meaningful. When the company was a division of a major corporation, however, management was told what new products they were supposed to develop. In addition, they were asked to prepare return-on-investment statistics and budgets showing that the proposed products would be extremely successful. The vice president was told to manipulate the sales and cost data in any way necessary to make central management's pet project appear successful. Because this was a common practice, marketing management paid no heed to accounting data. Now, however, the marketing manager recognizes the value of accounting information based on reasonable projections.

Summary

The S Co. operates in a unique industry. Government regulations are not important, but rulemaking bodies and safety factors are important considerations. The company differs from most of the others discussed in that many new products are brought to the company by independent inventors. In addition, advertising plays a role in an early stage of the decision process.

Once the subjective criteria have been used to reduce the number of possible new products, the objective data enter the picture in the form of return-on-investment statistics. Nonfinancial objectives sometimes will overrule the financial objectives, particularly if equipment for children is involved. The company has introduced a great number of new products in recent years, and these have, for the most part, been quite successful.

Paper Products Company

Paper Products Company is a New England-based manufacturer of industrial and consumer paper products. The company is listed on the New York Stock Exchange and is one of the leaders in its field. The person ultimately responsible for new products is the divisional vice president. Reporting to the vice president are the directors of marketing, engineering, and R&D. Under these three directors are 40 individuals whose sole duties are related to new-product innovation and development. These 40 hold the title of product-line specialists. The company intentionally has avoided giving these people the title of new-product managers although the vice president says they would have that title in other companies. The vice president is reluctant to call the individuals managers for fear they will place more effort on supervision of subordinates than on creativity. He also does not want to use the phrase "new product" in their title for fear they will stress new products and ignore adaptation of old products. There is no stereotype of product-line specialists. Because their primary responsibility is creativity, any educational background is acceptable. Some product-line specialists have engineering backgrounds, others are chemists, and still others have degrees in marketing and finance. The job descriptions of the product-line specialists intentionally are obscure. Basically, their job is to create change.

The company's definition of new products is quite broad. It includes innovations, adaptations of old products, and development of new manufacturing processes. There is, however, no new-product policy manual. The vice president feels that prescribed policies are detrimental to the new-product development process because creativity takes place in a variety of environments. As innovation cannot be predicted, the company does not want to risk stifling a development because of arbitrary corporate policies.

The company had only one overall corporate objective, and that involves return on investment. The vice president told us that his goal for 1983 was to increase profits by $60 million. Of that, $15 million was designated as coming from new products.

Under the company's broad definition, there are usually at least 1,000 new products developed each year. Only about a dozen of these could be considered true innovations. The remainder are adaptations of old products and new manufacturing processes. The vice president estimated that about 8% of new products ultimately reached the market. The numbers quoted above are somewhat misleading in that they include both industrial and consumer products. Thus, a single innovation may count as two or more new products as it can be sold to both industrial customers and to consumers.

The New-Product Decision Process

The new-product decision process begins when an item is created in the R&D department. Usually there is no known use for the product. In other words, the company is first and foremost technology oriented. There is very little guidance offered the R&D staff relative to the types of products upon which they should be working. Idle capacity, however, sometimes enters the picture as R&D is occasionally told to concentrate effort on products which could be produced in a specific idle factory and on specific pieces of idle equipment. Once a product has been developed, the marketing department must figure out a use for the item and identify a potential market. Actually, the marketing department constantly monitors business trends and social changes in order to conceive ideas for new products. Therefore, the matching of the new technology to a specific market need sometimes is simply a matter of matching the work of the R&D department with the already completed work of the marketing staff.

If the R&D technology can be used to develop a product identified by marketing, engineering then converts the technology from the lab to the production line in conjunction with the financial staff. The financial people are familiar enough with the production process to constantly ask questions and make recommendations regarding capital equipment to be acquired and labor processes to be used.

Once the production line has been designed fully, the expected return on investment is calculated. Sensitivity analysis is used, as are learning curves and a variety of assumptions for competitor reactions. The vice president identified the computation of return on investment as the key point in the decision process. Because corporate goals are involved solely with return on investment, any products not meeting such goals will be abandoned regardless of technological superiority. The vice president stated that the company may be technology oriented, but management knows that the income statement is the only true measure of success.

If a new product appears to have the potential for success, the company goes into production and places the product on the market. Sometimes the company starts slowly with new products by introducing them in only a few regions of the country. This gives production management time to get the bugs out of the production line and gives marketing a chance to get a feel for how successful the product will be.

The new-product development process is monitored by Gantt charts. Once developed, the new product is monitored by the new-product staff until it reaches the beginning of the maturity stage of its life cycle. At that point, the product is turned over to a regular product-line manager for routine monitoring. During the introductory and growth stages, the new product is watched closely via special monthly reports showing sales and gross profit by product and by region. These special reports are discontinued after a product reaches the maturity stage of its life cycle.

In summary, the go, no-go decision has to be made at the following points:

1. During the R & D process,
2. Following the development of a product by R & D,
3. Following the matching of an R & D development and a need identified by marketing,
4. Following the computation of return on investment,
5. During the introductory and growth stages of the life cycle.

The first of the above decision points occurs within the R & D department. The R & D director is solely responsible for the products his department will develop. There is no outside interference other than budget constraints, so an abandonment within the R & D department may be caused by either a lack of promise (in the view of the R & D director) or by a shortage of budgeted funds. The director can request additional funds if they are needed to complete a particularly important project. Such requests are evaluated at the corporate level along with similar requests from other divisions.

Once a product has been developed by R & D, it is turned over to the marketing staff. The marketing director can veto any development on the grounds that there is no known market for the item (point 2 above). If the marketing director feels an item has potential, the new product and opinions of the marketing staff are turned over to the vice president, who makes the subjective decision of whether to proceed (point 3). If the vice president likes the product, and the engineering budget will permit that department to work on another product, then the new item is turned over to engineering and finance. Members of the engineering and finance departments work together to develop the most efficient and effective production line. The return on investment is computed, and the vice president decides whether to introduce the product.

Actually this decision (point 4) is quite complex because the vice president is presented with a number of return-on-investment statistics that have been prepared using sensitivity analysis. Even the possible actions of competitors are included in the return-on-investment model.

After a product has been introduced, it is monitored for several months by the new-product staff and by the vice president. If the product does not respond as expected during the introductory and growth stages, it will be taken off the market.

The vice president emphasized that an abandonment at any point is not necessarily permanent. The company keeps files on all products abandoned. Future changes in the economic or societal environment may make today's abandonment a future success. Also, no one seemed to have any idea what the abandonment rate was at any point in the decision process.

Although return on investment is the primary consideration, the company does have nonfinancial objectives. The first of these is to not pollute the environment—even though such pollution may be legal. The other nonfinancial objective is to continue operating manufacturing plants in those communities where the company has historically played an important role. In essence, the nonfinancial objectives can be summarized with the phrase, "to be a good corporate citizen."

Assessment of Accounting Data

In general, the vice president was quite enthusiastic about the company's accountants. He described them as go-getters who could ask the right questions and contribute to the new-product development process. He also mentioned their use of sophisticated tools such as sensitivity analysis, learning curves, and decision trees. Although he mentioned budget constraints as a problem, he said the accountants were not to blame as the budgets start with those people who will be affected by them.

As an illustration of the accountants' work, the vice president discussed a recent product in which he and the three directors thought a new technology would revolutionize the industry and have a lasting impact on the company. The accountants responded that they had heard that story before, but their studies showed that no previous technologies had lasted more than 12 years. Thus, they would not compute ROI statistics for any life expectancy greater than 12 years. The top managers could not dispute the accountants' findings, so there is now an unwritten rule that life expectancies of new products will never exceed 12 years—no matter how revolutionary.

Summary

Paper Products is technology oriented. New products start with innovation, and only later are the possible consumers considered. This emphasis on product first and possible market second naturally results in a decision process somewhat different from those companies discussed previously.

Paper Products has one of the largest (if not the largest) organizations devoted to new-product development of any company interviewed in this study. However, there is no new-product policy manual, and there are no written job descriptions for new-product staff members. These deviations from what most people would consider good management practice apparently are due to the emphasis on creativity as opposed to routine market analysis.

In conclusion, the company's new-product development process is technically oriented, but the secret to the company's success with new products is attributable to the team concept. A tremendous range of talents is necessary to develop a new product. Scientists, marketers, engineers, and accountants all play important roles in the new-product decision process.

Midwest Brewing Company

Of all of the companies included in this research project, Midwest Brewing Company (B Co.) has the narrowest product line and definition of new products. B Co. is one of the largest brewers in the nation, but essentially it has only one product—beer. The company's definition of new products is simple—new brands of beer. Generally, the goals of the new-product department are to segment the beer market, then develop beer brands that will cater to the desires of the identified market segment.

The new-product manager reports to the director of marketing, who subsequently reports to the vice president of marketing. The new-product manager and the director of marketing make abandonment decisions. The new-product manager works on about 10 ideas each year, but only one of these ideas is introduced nationally. The introduction of one per year is a result of budget limitations, and the costs of advertising a new product are so great that only the product ranked as best by the new-product manager will be marketed nationally.

The new-product decision process is codified to some extent in a policy manual. Most of the guidelines are constraints imposed by master brewers and manufacturers of cans and bottles. There are no ROI or payback guidelines, but gross profit percentage is a consideration. Another criterion is that available manufacturing capacity must be available to allow production time for any new brand.

The New-Product Decision Process

As mentioned above, a new product is a new brand that will appeal to a certain segment of the beer-buying market. Initially ideas may come from the company's regular product brand managers who submit their ideas to the new-product manager. Alternatively, the new-product manager may create his own ideas based on concept studies performed by a marketing research firm. If ideas are originated by brand managers or other employees, the company uses concept studies to determine the feasibility of the product idea. It should be noted that there is a reward system within the company to encourage all employees to submit new-product ideas. The new-product manager also watches the activities of competitors. If a competitor identifies a market segment, B Co. will seek that segment as well. In other words, the company is both an innovator and an imitator.

The company designs a concept study to determine what beer drinkers like and dislike about the beers they presently drink. Questions relate to such factors as taste, caloric content, color, price, and size of cans and bottles. In other words, the concept studies explore the ways in which the company can slightly alter its beer and appeal to a specific audience.

Using the concept study as a basis, the new-product manager either develops an idea for a product or approves a previously defined idea. After the director of marketing approves the idea, the new-product manager proceeds. The marketing director's decision is based on the marketing research data provided by the new-product manager. The specifications for the new product then are given to the R & D staff, who produces a beer that meets the desired specifications.

The new-product manager's next decision is whether to test market the new beer. If the decision is to proceed, the next steps involve selecting a name, designing a package, and devising advertising strategy for the new brand. These are significant steps because image is very important to beer drinkers. Usually beers must have a "macho" name and package design. Also, the name must be memorable and have impact. The advertising strategies must combine macho characters with those who are believable.

Once the above steps are completed, the new product is introduced in six test market areas. Two different prices are used in the test markets to determine price elasticity. Test market reports include the volume of sales and the buyers. The company is concerned with the buyers because of the problem with cannibalization of other company brands.

On the average, about two new products survive the test market stage each year. The next step is for the new-product manager to rank the successful products and get approval from the director of marketing to introduce the product nationally. Those products that are not introduced may begin the evaluation process over again in a future year. Once a product has been introduced nationally, it leaves the administration of the new-product department.

The final ranking is essentially an objective decision, but there are some subjective elements. For example, market share percentage sometimes is considered as distributors are less likely to push an item that has a small market share precentage, regardless of dollar volume. The company feels that being a big factor in a small market is more important than being only a small contributor in a large market. The new-product manager states that being big in a market adds visibility to the company.

The go, no-go decisions in B Co's. new-product decision process can be summarized as occurring at the following points:

1. Following the completion of concept studies,
2. Following completion of R & D work,
3. Following test marketing,
4. Following the ranking of products which have been successful in the test market.

The abandonment rate after step 1 above usually is about 50%. An additional 30% are abandoned by the end of step 3. Thus, for every 10 ideas, only about two remain to be ranked in step 4. Then one new product is introduced annually. The abandonment decisions are made by the new-product manager, but the approval of the director of marketing is required at decision steps 1 and 4. With the exception of step 2, the decisions are based on objective data—expected gross profit percentage. Step 2 is based on taste.

Assessment of Accounting Data

Most of the new-product decision process at B Co. is based on marketing research data. With the exception of expected gross profit percentage, there is little reliance on accounting data. The accounting staff, however, is responsible for translating marketing research data into gross profit percentages. The new-product manager states that the accountants are quite capable and "are better at manipulating numbers than most people." He says that he has to rely heavily on the accountants' treatment of marketing research data because all upper management wants to know is the bottom line.

Summary

B Co. is unusual in that it deals in only one product category, and any new products are simply an altered version of an existing product. It relies heavily on marketing research data, and return-on-investment data are limited to the computation of gross profit percentage. As important as the product itself is the image that product conveys. Consequently, brand name and advertising strategies are important considerations. Also unusual is the fact that B Co. limits its new-product introductions to one per year. Even if a second product meets the financial guidelines, that product is abandoned in favor of the better product. Of course this treatment could be in reality an unofficial form of sensitivity analysis. Given the same risks, the product showing the greater return is the one marketed.

Canadian Food Products Company

Canadian Food Products Company (CF Co.) is a large subsidiary of a European corporation. Although the company aims its products at the mass market, it considers its products to be of only the highest quality. The company's definition of new products is divided into two categories—line extensions and truly new products. Both types of new products are handled in the same way except that the truly new products require extra effort in the areas of selecting a brand name and an advertising strategy. When asked whether the company has a new-product policy manual, both the group product manager and the product manager said, "Probably— this company has a policy manual for everything. However, we have never seen it and do not use it."

The New-Product Decision Process

The group product manager intitiates new-product ideas. He discusses the ideas with his superior, the product manager, and together they come to a decision as to whether to proceed. The next step is to submit the ideas to the division manager, who reports to the corporate president in Europe.

The managers are quite candid about their source of ideas. All ideas are imitations of successful U.S. products. The group product manager, who has a liaison person at the company's sister subsidiary in the United States, makes four trips a year to the United States for purposes of generating new ideas for the Canadian company. He comes away not only with the ideas, but also with U.S. sales figures. These sales figures ultimately are submitted to the division manager, along with estimates for the Canadian market, as support for producing the new products. The product manager could think of no instance in which an idea for a new product had been generated internally. Employees are not asked for suggestions—there is no suggestion box—nor is there any reward system for new ideas.

One of the primary considerations of the product manager involves product positioning. His judgment is required as to whether a new product would cannibalize the company's present line. If the possibility of cannibalization seems small, then the product manager looks at the financial data.

Before asking the division manager to approve a new-product idea, the product manager compiles estimated sales figures, costs, expected profit margins, and market share statistics. This is usually the extent of the data as most new products are produced using present capacity. If a capital investment is required, the process is expanded because engineering then will determine the best means of getting the necessary equipment into service. The financial staff provides the ROI figures.

Market share percentage is another important consideration because distributors are unwilling to handle products with small shares of the market. Thus, a product that otherwise might be profitable sometimes has to be abandoned because of a small market share.

Once the division manager gives the go-ahead, the idea is turned over to R & D for development. The subsequent product is then test marketed in two cities, using different advertising strategies. The resulting profit margins under each strategy are evaluated to determine which would be preferable for the national introduction.

The test market is considered successful if the profits meet the previously established expectations.

The company makes no estimates of price elasticity during the test marketing of a product. Instead, during the idea stage the product manager establishes a price-point based on what he thinks the market will bear. The product subsequently is priced at that arbitrary amount.

Following successful test marketing, a product is introduced nationally. The company tracks the new product for one year to be certain that it is meeting expectations, although managers have never tried to do any analysis of why failures have occurred.

CF Co. occasionally will allow nonfinancial objectives to override a decision based on financial objectives. For example, unprofitable line extensions sometimes are used to block competitors' introductions from a particular market.

There are no ecological considerations that influence new-product development. Social responsibility, however, does because the company wants to be involved with only high-quality products. Government regulation also plays a role. Approval is required for packages and labels, and the company's meat processing department is subject to meat inspection laws.

In summary, the go, no-go decisions are made at the following points at CF Co:

1. After a consideration of product positioning,
2. After comparision to profitability criteria (margin, ROI, and payback),
3. After consideration of market share percentage,
4. After development by R & D,
5. After test marketing.

Essentially the product manager makes all these decisions, although the division manager must approve all "go" decisions from step 2 on. In other words, approval is necessary in order to spend more money, but no approval is required for abandonments.

All the above decision points are judgment decisions essentially, except number 5. Even though points 2 and 3 are based on objective data, the figures are only estimates. Decision point 4 (after development by R & D) is based partially on judgment (Is the product tasty?) and partially on objective data (Can product be produced to sell at the desired price?). Of all ideas considered initially, only about 10% make it through step 3. Of those that are turned over to R & D, only 20 to 40% survive steps 4 and 5.

Assessment of Accounting Data

The accounting department provides all profit margin and ROI figures. Budgeted financial statements for a prospective new product are prepared for 18 years into the future. In fact, the product manager feels he is inundated with excessive accounting data. Budget reports are prepared in extreme detail with full explanation of how every number has been determined. Unfortunately, there never is any analysis of the resulting data. The accountants are strictly "numbers crunchers" who provide no analytical feedback.

The product manager has no criticism of the quality of the data provided, other than the extreme detail. He says that he is concerned only with the bottom line, not with how data are generated. He would particularly like to see from accounting the important numbers supported by an analysis of how the budgeted figures compare to the industry norms and corporate objectives. He also would like to know how the key figures could be manipulated by changing the marketing mix. One thing about the accounting data which the product manager does like is that new products utilizing previously idle capacity do not have to bear their full share of overhead allocations during the first year. This setup permits manufacturing to get through the high-cost phases of the learning curve before full overhead allocations are made.

Summary

CF Co. is completely dependent upon the U.S. market for generating new-product ideas. All new products are imitations of U.S.-made products. This philosophy is justified because Canadian consumers usually are not considered (by the product manager) as avant-garde as U.S. consumers. Thus, the company reduces its new-product risk by producing only items that have been successful in the United States.

The new-product decision process at CF Co. is centered around estimated sales figures. Estimates are based on actual results in the United States. Subsequently, test market results are compared to the predetermined estimates. Even the profit margins and ROI figures are based on the estimated level of sales. No quantitative models of any type are used.

Despite its lack of true innovation, CF Co. has prospered and is one of Canada's largest and most profitable food processing companies. Actual sales and profit figures, however, are not divulged to the public.

Canadian Sporting Goods

Canadian Sporting Goods (CS Co.), a wholly owned subsidiary of a U.S. corporation, is the leading producer of sporting equipment in Canada. The company's definition of new products includes anything that is new to the company—even color changes or new sizes. CS Co. is unique among the companies in this study in that new-product decisions are made by a product development commmittee (PDC). The committee is composed of the president, sales manager, product manager, chief tooling engineer, chief design engineer, manufacturing chief, and secretary/treasurer. Other people can be added for specific products. All new products—even color changes—must filter through the PDC, which meets monthly.

CS Co. does not have a new-product policy manual or anything else in writing, but it does have an unwritten procedure that is quite structured. The entire process is independent of the parent company except when a large sum is necessary for capital expenditures. The impression was given, however, that investments requiring large capital expenditures were rarely made in order to avoid going to the parent.

The New-Product Decision Process

Ideas for new products originate from a number of sources. Dozens of ideas are received each year from consumers who urge the company to manufacture a specific item. Other ideas are generated internally—primarily by design engineers. Whatever the source, no one receives a reward or extra pay. Another source of ideas is the minutes of PDC meetings held at other company divisions throughout the world. Every PDC is required to send its minutes to the PDCs in other countries. The divisions do not really work together on new products, but corporate management feels that creativity is enhanced if PDC members have a basic idea of what is going on at other divisions. This concept of exchanging minutes is based on the idea of cross-pollination rather than imitation. Basically, the company considers itself innovative rather than imitative.

Ideas for new products can be submitted to any member of the PDC. If the PDC member likes the idea, he brings it before the entire committee. If the committee likes the idea, the concept enters the evaluation stage of the product development process. During the evaluation stage, the marketing department conducts surveys to determine the market potential for a prospective product. At the same time, the accounting staff works with engineering and manufacturing to develop estimated cost figures. Once all the data have been put together, the results are presented to the PDC and a decision is made whether to proceed. The important criteria include ROI, payback, gross margin percentage, market share percentage, and contribution margin percentage. Possible distribution channels also are considered; a product marketed outside the company's normal channels would have to show much higher returns than a product marketed through normal channels. It also was mentioned that seasonal products must show higher returns than year-around products.

Another important consideration during the evaluation stage is the existence of idle capacity. Because the company wants to avoid asking the parent for investment capital, products which either utilize idle capacity or are labor intensive receive preferential treatment. It was explained that capital equipment is much higher priced in Canada than the United States. Thus, labor-intensive manufacturing processes usually are more profitable than capital-intensive methods. Consequently, products made in Canada rarely are identical to products made by the parent corporation in the United States, even when the products are used for the same purposes.

The second stage of the development process is the design stage in which models are developed. Key factors at this point include product quality and safety. Also, most products must meet government regulations and pass government inspections. Packaging also is considered during the design stage. When the finished model is presented to the PDC for approval, cost estimates are re-evaluated to determine whether they still seem reasonable.

When a model has been approved, the manufacturing department gears up to produce a trial run (usually 500 units). It uses the critical path method to coordinate the setup in the manufacturing department. These trial units are given to consumers for field testing. The reports submitted by the testing consumers are evaluated by the PDC before the company decides on national introduction. The company has never used test marketing; the trial units are always given to consumers. The field-test reports usually result in a few minor product changes to improve the product. Once the improvements are made, the PDC makes the final decision regarding introduction.

Once a product has been introduced nationally, the PDC monitors it for two years through the regular financial reports. Special reports for new products are not necessary. The PDC evaluates rare failures in the marketplace for cause.

Occasionally the company considers nonfinancial objectives when evaluating a new-product idea. Specifically, they include producing a low-margin product to keep a competitor out of a market and producing an item in order to provide continued employment to employees in an old plant. In addition to safety and a dedication to high quality, these were the only social objectives noted. Problems with ecology never have been a consideration.

CS Co. has not conducted any tests of price elasticity although it surveys salesmen during the evaluation stage to determine their opinions regarding price elasticity.

The go, no-go decisions are made at the following points at CS Co.:

1. Following consideration of an idea by a single member of the product development committee,
2. Following an evaluation of the merits of a new-product concept,
3. After the product has been designed and costs re-evaluated,
4. After a trial run in manufacturing and a field test of the trial units.

The decisions at steps 2, 3, and 4 are made by the committee as a whole. Essentially, the company says it has a three-stage product development process. Each of the three stages (evaluation, design, and manufacturing) is quite involved and includes a number of considerations.

About 50% of those ideas which the committee evaluates reach the trial manufacturing run. Approximately 75% of those reaching the manufacturing stage are introduced to the national market. Market failures are quite rare.

Assessment of Accounting Data

As discussed earlier, the accountants compute costs, ROI, payback, and profit margins. In addition, they are responsible for investigating patents and obtaining patents and copyrights. Finally, the accountants examine warranty statements, owner's manuals, and operating instructions to uncover areas of possible liability.

The only criticism of the accounting staff is the long delays involved in obtaining much of the needed information. The accounting figures are always accurate and helpful, but the accountants often delay the committee's activities.

Summary

CS Co. is unusual in that its new-product development program is controlled entirely by a standing committee. Apparently the concept is effective because the company is the leader in its field and has introduced a large number of new products in recent years.

Although CS Co. is a subsidiary of a U.S. corporation and even produces some of the same products as the parent, it is independent in virtually all other respects. Management at CS Co. says its products tend to be far different from and more innovative than those of the parent. The reason is different cost pressures in the two countries. Because capital equipment is either not easily available, or much more costly in Canada, the subsidiary relies more on labor-intensive manufacturing methods. These differences also mean that Canadian new products cannot be simply imitations of U.S. products. The differences in the environment require the subsidiary to be innovative.

Canadian Food Processors

Canadian Food Processors (CFP Co.) is a wholly owned subsidiary of a United States parent. Canadian sales are in excess of $200 million annually. A new product is defined as anything new to the company—even flavor changes. All activities are independent of the parent, but the parent has limited CFP's activities to the consumer food business. The only corporate-level objective deals with return on investment.

Although there are no formal policies concerning the development of new products, there is a standardized procedure that is followed. The development process involves a large number of people in a variety of departments.

The New-Product Decision Process

All ideas for new products are based on products already on the market in the United States and in Europe. Individuals at the vice president level make regular trips to food shows in the developed nations for purposes of finding new products. The company is strictly imitative—primarily because of the lower level of risk involved. Once a vice president has an idea with potential for the Canadian market, he submits it to the new-product development committee (NPDC) on a new-product development request form.

This NPDC is composed of high-level marketing and R & D people, including the director of the new-product development department. The company has never used product ideas received from customers, salespeople, or other employees.

The NPDC evaluates the idea and estimates potential sales. The accounting staff prepares cost estimates and does an ROI analysis. Gross profit margin goals also must be met. Payback, however, is not used because the company is concerned with long-term growth, not short-term results. Also, all new products must be made with current facilities. The existence of idle capacity is a primary consideration. If the NPDC likes the looks of the numbers, it sends the idea to the president for his approval or veto. If the president approves, the idea is turned over to the new-product development department (NPDD), which then contracts with the R & D group to develop a sample.

Once a sample has been developed, the product is taste tested in-house. If acceptable, the product is sent to independent testing labs where professional taste panels evaluate it. A favorable outcome is followed by in-home tests. The next step is to test market the product in a single city. If the test market is acceptable at the city level, it is expanded to a provincewide test market. After about a year, the company evaluates the provincewide results. If the product has met profit expectations, the market is expanded to a second province. Additional provinces are added—one at a time—as long as profit expectations are met. However, the product is transferred out of the NPDD and is no longer considered new after the market area has expanded beyond one province.

The company has one nonfinancial objective, but it has indirect financial implications. The company will not consider a new product unless management thinks the company can be number one in the market. The company says that a product needs a large market share to warrant the advertising necessary to entice large chain stores to carry the product. Five chains have nearly 85% of the Canadian grocery business. Thus, Canadian Food Processors must cater to these chains by providing heavy advertising support. Advertising is used during the test market period and at introduction. Little consideration is given to package design; the package is viewed strictly as an accessory.

The company has no other nonfinancial objectives. Ecology has never been a consideration, nor do government regulations play a role in the decision process. The company does work to be socially responsible by producing only healthy foods that will enable the consumer to maintain a balanced diet.

The company has not studied price elasticity. Because the company has the benefit of knowing the sales results of similar products in the United States, it usually prices the product comparable to U.S. products (even though the U.S. products are not necessarily marketed in Canada). CFP Co. uses no form of model or sophisticated quantitative tools other than the life-cycle model. Product life cycles are studied carefully with the objective of prolonging the life cycle as much as possible.

There are budget constraints on the new-product development process. The NPDD is subject to an annual budget. Once the budget limit has been reached, the NPDD cannot accept any more new-product requests for a particular year.

The NPDD does follow up on product failures. Actually, the follow-up process is ongoing. Every six months an assessment must be prepared for every product that is not meeting profit expectations. This is true both for the products in the city test market stage and those that have been introduced provincewide. Consequently, if a product ultimately is abandoned, the reason already has been reported in the semiannual reports of the NPDD. No special tools are necessary to monitor new-product sales because monthly financial statements already are prepared for every product. New products do bear their fair share of factory overhead.

The go, no-go decisions at CFP Co. can be summarized as occurring at the following points:

1. Following review by the new-product development committee,
2. Following review by the president,
3. Following in-house taste tests,
4. Following independent laboratory taste tests,
5. Following in-home taste tests,
6. Following citywide test market,
7. Following provincewide test market.

The first decision point centers around both objective opinions of the product and profitability potential. Decision points 3, 4, and 5 are based primarily on taste, but costs are recomputed at every stage to be sure the product still seems profitable. Of all products surviving the first decision point, about 80% reach the test market stage. Of those products test marketed, about 50% subsequently are introduced beyond a single province.

Assessment of Accounting Data

There was no criticism of the accounting data, but there was one suggestion that merits consideration. It seems that people in the new-product development department tend to view the accountants' estimates as being exact. It would be preferable for the accountants' estimates of costs to be presented as a range rather than as single, precise figures. In practice, the cost estimates typically are within 25% of actual costs, but many product ideas are abandoned because they fail to meet profit margin goals by only a fraction of a percent. Range estimates would help marketing people understand that costs cannot be predetermined exactly.

Summary

CFP Co. is strictly an imitator. Nothing indicates that this philosophy has anything to do with the company being a subsidiary of a U.S. corporation. In fact, it copies European products as well as American ones.

The company does have a unique system (at least among companies in this study) in that a committee initially evaluates new-product ideas. Subsequently, the idea is turned over to a new-product department, and the role of the committee is finished. Also, the president is given an opportunity to veto every idea before development begins. Perhaps because of the number of people involved and the fact that the company is an imitator, its success rate is quite high.

Canadian Wines, Ltd.

Canadian Wines, Ltd. (CW Co.) is one of Canada's largest vintners, operating wineries in most provinces. The company is public and listed on several large stock exchanges. Wine is the company's only product. Most sales are made in Canada although some exports are made to the United States, Great Britain, and Japan. The company's products have won numerous international awards of excellence. All manufacturing operations are in Canada, but the company operates importing subsidiaries in other countries.

CW Co.'s definition of a new product is anything it does not produce currently, and it has no formal policies covering new products. The company's operations basically are decentralized. Each individual winery is a profit center. However, the decision to introduce a new product requires approval at both the division and corporate levels.

The New-Product Decision Process

Ideas for new products usually originate with someone reading a wine magazine—either the general manager (top officer) of a winery or the marketing manager at the corporate level. The originator submits his idea to the other individual for approval. Both the marketing manager and a general manager must agree before a new product can be introduced. The company uses this centralized planning to avoid individual divisions bottling wines that would compete with each other.

CW Co. is strictly an imitator. Managers subscribe to a variety of wine industry magazines for purposes of discovering trends in the industry which can result in the success of new products. If a market segment is discovered anywhere in the world in which the company has no products, a new-product idea is generated. The company believes that the Canadian wine consumer is similar to other wine consumers throughout the world.

The marketing manager and division general manager jointly estimate the potential Canadian market for the new product. Based on these market estimates, accountants prepare prospective profit figures. If the financial statements look promising, the decision is made to produce the new product. No return-on-investment calculations are made, primarily because no capital investments are made. All new products must be produced with idle capacity. Occasionally a new product will be packaged in a newly designed bottle, and the mold for this bottle requires a capital investment. Under this circumstance, which is rare, the chief financial officer must approve the expenditure.

Once the marketing manager and general manager have agreed on a new product, the next step is to design a label for the wine bottles. Label design is considered the most important step in the development of a new product because it must define the personality of the wine. Label design is the only major cost in the development of most new products.

Creating the new product is not a problem. Managers simply inform the vintners of the desired recipe, then they mix the grapes in the proper proportions. R & D plays no role in the development of a new product. The taste of the new product is not even a major consideration. Vintners typically conduct taste tests to be certain that their mixture does indeed match the wine they are trying to imitate. The company, however, has never conducted any form of outside taste tests, consumer surveys, or other types of tests because the costs of getting into the market are so low. Most surveys would cost more than it costs to introduce a new product. It typically takes CW Co. about six months to go from an idea to shipping the product, but that period has been as short as two months. As mentioned, the only cause for delay is the need for designing an appropriate label.

The company does not support new products with advertising. This philosophy, however, is a major issue within the company. The marketing manager feels advertising would be very helpful. The president and board of directors, though, are opposed to advertising. Consequently, sales are entirely dependent upon the work of the sales representatives and word-of-mouth advertising. The marketing manager noted that a competitor has been increasing its market share at the company's expense in recent years by using heavy doses of advertising.

The company monitors the progress of a new product and established products by means of monthly financial statements prepared on an item-by-item basis. No other models or quantitative tools are used. The company does not even analyze price elasticity. Prices are always set so that they will be slightly lower than those of competitors.

Profit margin is the criterion new products have to meet. There are no nonfinancial objectives, no safety considerations, and no problems concerning ecology. Even social aspects are not considered. The marketing manager admitted that wineries could not do much boasting in the areas of social concerns or ecology, so the company keeps quiet on those subjects. Even market share percentage is not a major criterion, although at least a percent or two is necessary to induce retailers to carry the brands.

Surprisingly, the company has little problem with government regulations even though all domestic sales are made to government liquor boards. These boards limit the times when beverage manufacturers can introduce new products or make deletions from their lines to two dates per year, but they do not limit the number of new products that can be added at one time or the number that can be deleted. CW Co. performs no analysis of why products fail.

The new-product decision process at CW Co. is quite simple, and the go, no-go decision is made at only one point—after evaluation of the profit potential. The decision is a joint one involving the corporate-level marketing manager and a division-level general manager. The decision is based on profit estimates generated by the accounting staff. The estimates are based on a given price and predicted sales volume. About 60% of all ideas generated eventually are marketed as new products.

Assessment of Accounting Data

The marketing manager was unhappy with the data provided by the accounting staff. Profit projections involve full allocation of overhead to new products—even when considerable idle capacity exists. Incremental costs and revenues would be a more practical means of measuring the profit contribution of a new product. As it now stands, a new product may be reported as unprofitable, but total profits of the division will increase because a favorable volume variance will be generated by adding the new product.

Fortunately, the general managers are aware of this situation and usually ignore the work of the accountants—or at least revise the figures to determine the effect on total profits. The general managers and marketing manager, however, do not always have the data necessary to revise the accountants' figures correctly. Consequently, it would be preferable if the accountants would present estimated statements on an incremental basis rather than on an average cost basis.

Summary

CW Co. is similar to the brewery discussed earlier in that it produces only one product, and new items are based on segmentations of the market. At CW, profit margin is the only criterion for acceptance of a new product (given that idle capacity exists). No capital investment is required, and there is no difficulty in developing the new product. Essentially, the only thing difficult about the entire development process is what type of label will appear on the bottle. Everything else is viewed as given—or so low cost that no real decision is necessary. Even advertising is avoided.

Although the new-product development process may seem overly simplified, it cannot be criticized. The company has trebled its sales over the past decade, enjoying increases each year.

Canadian Building Supplies, Ltd.

Canadian Building Supplies, Ltd. is a large manufacturer of building supplies sold directly to consumers and industrial customers. The company is listed on several stock exchanges and has numerous plants throughout Canada. Because of the large size of many of the company's products, it is usually cheaper to manufacture near the ultimate customer rather than ship products long distances. Consequently, many of the plants are similar in terms of types of products.

Canadian Building Supplies has no formal new-product policy manual. No one has a definition of new products other than something not currently being marketed, but there is a uniform system that is typically followed before a new product goes into production.

The New-Product Decision Process

The company's sales managers initiate ideas for new products. These ideas normally are based on products already successful in the United States or ones that are being marketed by competitors in Canada. The company is strictly imitative and introduces new products only when there is a potential for capturing a large market share in an already established market. The marketing vice president cited the small size of the Canadian market as being a deterrent to spending money on innovative research.

After informal discussion with the marketing vice president, the sales manager prepares a formal new-product proposal, which includes estimates of sales volume and a rough financial analysis. The proposal is submitted to several vice presidents for analysis: those in charge of marketing, production, engineering, finance, and environmental control. The purpose of the analysis is to revise the proposal. The vice presidents try to anticipate every cost that might be incurred if the proposed product were produced, not only manufacturing costs, but also those related to packaging and distribution. After obtaining input from all departments, the vice president of marketing submits a revised proposal to the group. Additional revisions then may be made. The financial vice president is the last person to review the proposal, and he provides the final estimates of ROI and payback. The marketing vice president makes this the ultimate decision whether to proceed. This entire analysis process takes about six months.

The analysis of new-product proposals is done typically with pen and ink. If a capital investment of more than $1 million is involved, however, the accountants prepare the ROI and payback calculations by means of a sensitivity and risk analysis computer program. A linear programming transportation model also is used to determine which plant, or plants, will manufacture the new products. Opinion studies of price elasticity occasionally have been conducted by the marketing department to obtain inputs for the sensitivity analysis model.

As mentioned, one of the company's major considerations is environmental control. For example, because of foul-smelling emissions, new plants typically are built far out in the "boondocks" to avoid problems with unhappy neighbors. Such locations, however, usually require higher transportation costs. Another example of an ecological consideration was given in which certain machinery at one old plant gives off such foul odors that the plant operates only when the wind is coming from the north. (Apparently there are no neighbors to the south of the plant, or maybe it is located near the U.S. border.) Such considerations must be incorporated into the decision to introduce a new product.

The financial analysis of a proposal is based on incremental costs and revenues. Consequently, more new products are introduced during times of idle capacity than at other times because the new products do not have to absorb any fixed overhead. Although the company said it had no nonfinancial objectives for new products, the vice president pointed out that the utilization of idle capacity sometimes was a consideration in introducing a new product.

Government regulations play a minor role in the decision process at Canadian Building Supplies. If a new plant is to be built, however, the company usually will put it in an area of high unemployment because the government will provide monetary incentives for providing employment in the less prosperous areas.

Although the company does not have a formal test marketing program, it obtains some of the benefits of test marketing in that only one plant is used initially to manufacture a new product. Because of high transportation costs, the use of only one plant effectively regionalizes the introduction of a product. For the first year after introduction, the marketing vice president closely monitors the progress of new products by means of the regular product-line financial statements. Actual sales are compared to the sales estimated in the original proposal. The company has never conducted follow-up studies to determine the reason why products have failed.

Budget constraints play no role in the consideration of new products. Budgets can be revised for any good reason, and a product that promises a positive return on investment is the best possible reason to revise a budget.

Although a great deal of analysis takes place before the decision is made to manufacture a new product, there is only one decision point and one decision maker. Once the analysis of a new-product proposal has gone through several cycles and revised ROI and payback data have been calculated, the marketing vice president makes the go, no-go decision.

The entire decision process sounds quite sophisticated, but we were doubtful of the need for all that analysis after we learned what portion of new-product ideas actually survived the analysis process. We were told that about 99% of all ideas eventually are introduced nationally. In effect, putting through the proposal paperwork is nothing more than a formality. We were told that ideas for new products are not generated until they are highly successful for competitors, so CB Co. simply makes a similar product to accomplish the same purpose.

Assessment of Accounting Data

The accounting staff provides a great deal of sophisticated data, particularly when a proposal includes a request for capital funds in excess of $1 million. In these situations, sensitivity and risk analysis are incorporated into the ROI and payback projections. In addition, transportation models are used in making all new-product decisions.

The company has only one criticism of its accountants. It says they should prepare special worksheet forms for the proposal analysis group because the necessity for constantly changing the cost estimates is the primary cause of a six-month delay in the analysis process. There is also some question as to why the sensitivity and risk analysis computer program could be used only in the analysis of large investments. The excuse is that the accountants are too busy to perform the analysis very often.

Summary

Canadian Building Supplies has a rather sophisticated analysis system followed by a single decision point at which the marketing vice president decides whether to proceed. The decision rarely results in an abandonment. The reason for the high success ratio is because the company is strictly an imitator which copies products already being produced in either the United States or Canada.

Canadian Glass & Plastics, Ltd.

Canadian Glass & Plastics, Ltd. (CG Co.) is one of Canada's oldest and largest manufacturers of glass containers. The company acquired a plastics subsidiary during the 1960s, and that product area now accounts for nearly one-fourth of the company's sales. CG Co. has manufacturing plants throughout Canada and operates wholly owned subsidiaries in the United States and Australia. Annual sales total about $250 million, and shares are traded on the major Canadian stock exchanges.

Although some of the company's products can be defined as true consumer products, the majority of items produced cannot be classified as strictly consumer or industrial because the immediate customer is an industrial firm which packages its own products in the containers produced by Canadian Glass. The ultimate user of CG Co.'s products, however, is the consumer. Philosophically, the management at CG Co. considers all the company's offerings as consumer products. Thus, surveys regarding user needs are conducted with individual consumers and not with the industries which actually buy the goods.

Canadian Glass has no new-product policy manual nor is any one person ultimately responsible for new products. Five product managers are responsible for developing new products which will ultimately become a part of their line. The company's definition of new products includes three types of items: (1) a product new to the company which is to be introduced into an existing market, (2) a product new to the company which is to be introduced into a new market, and (3) an existing product which is to be introduced into a new market. All three types of new products go through the same decision process.

The New-Product Decision Process

Ideas for new products come from a variety of sources, such as individual salesmen or other employees. Most come from semiannual new-product seminars in which product managers and salesmen discuss new ideas. Before the seminars, salesmen visit grocery stores to study every product that is not packaged in glass or the company's plastic containers and visualize whether each product *could* be packaged in CG Co.'s containers. Similar new-product seminars are held periodically with other groups of employees throughout the company. There is no formal reward system for employees suggesting new products, but employees are considered a valuable source of new ideas.

Ideas generated at these new-product seminars are divided among the product managers, who then make monthly reports to the marketing director regarding the progress of each idea. It is hard to say whether the company is innovative or imitative. The marketing director feels the company is innovative, but many products are glass imitations of metal containers. Thus, are such products innovative or imitative?

The company occasionally receives ideas from a large U.S. glass manufacturer with which it has an R&D technical assistance agreement. The U.S. corporation conducts the research, but Canadian Glass has full licensing rights. This agreement is primarily a source of new technology rather than specific product ideas.

Once a product manager has obtained an idea, he conducts a preliminary investigation of its profit potential and market size. The preliminary investigation typically includes interviews with consumers and grocery store managers concerning the perceived advantages of the product idea. Market size is a key factor because the company is oriented to high volume products. Thousands of containers can be produced on a single machine every hour, and management wants to be able to operate a set of molds for at least 72 hours (three days) at a stretch. Setup costs are quite high, so low-volume products usually are viewed as unprofitable. If after the analysis is complete the product manager still likes the idea, he passes it along to the design engineering review committee, who determines whether the company can manufacture the product with its present technology. This step is critical because the company is not capable of producing all types of containers. CG Co. is volume oriented, so all products must be capable of being made easily and quickly.

If the design engineers approve the product concept, then the accountants are called in to provide precise estimates of manufacturing costs. These cost estimates are combined with a selling price that has been predetermined by the product manager to calculate estimated gross profit margins, ROI, and payback figures. Payback must be two years or less.

If the product manager still likes the profit potential of the concept after seeing the accountants' figures, he places an order for the molds needed to manufacture the product. A set of molds typically costs about $15,000, and there is about a four-month lead time before the molds are delivered. If a capital investment is needed beyond the cost of molds (for example, a new factory building), the investment decision becomes more involved and requires the approval of the corporate president.

During the four-month wait for molds, the company develops advertisements and sends them to company salesmen. Ads also appear in grocery and hardware trade publications. Salesmen are given a date to start taking orders, and once the company receives the molds, it begins production.

CG Co. has some nonfinancial objectives for new products, such as maintaining an image of being a reliable supplier for container products. Thus, if a customer wants to expand a line with a new size of product, Canadian Glass will produce that container even though the volume of sales is too small to meet normal profit margins. The company also will accept lower-than-normal margins on export business if there is idle manufacturing capacity.

Ecology is a big selling point for the company's glass products because glass can be recycled, an advantage over products made of metal. The company tries to be a socially responsible corporate citizen by maintaining recycling centers throughout Canada. These recycling centers have two purposes: (1) to promote good government and public relations and (2) to provide crushed glass for producing new products at a cost lower than it would be using raw materials such as sand.

Government regulations sometimes have affected the new-product decision. The primary example includes the imposition of taxes on nonreturnable containers. Such a tax is beneficial to the company in that Canadian Glass produces better quality bottles that can be reused many times.

The company uses the critical path method to monitor progress of a new product once it decides to order molds. It also uses computer models to determine the quantity of items to be produced at any given time.

Once a new product has been introduced on the market, it is monitored for one year via special quarterly reports showing actual versus budgeted results. No follow-up studies are conducted to determine why failures have occurred. No studies or test markets are conducted to determine price elasticity either, but because most new products are replacements for metal or other types of containers, the product manager does know the maximum price which can be charged.

The go, no-go decisions at Canadian Glass can be summarized as occurring at the following points:

1. After preliminary investigation by the product manager,
2. After evaluation by the design engineering review committee,
3. After calculation of estimated costs, ROI, and payback.

The first and third decision points are the responsibility of the product manager. The design engineering review committee makes the decision at point 2. In addition, if large capital investments are required (more than just molds), the go decision at the third point must be approved by the marketing director and the corporate president. The marketing director estimates that about 5% of ideas initially evaluated reach the market. Very few fail once they do reach the market.

Assessment of Accounting Data

The duties of the accounting staff include the preparation of cost estimates and ROI data necessary for the product manager to make a decision regarding a new product. Once an item goes into production, the accountants prepare quarterly reports comparing estimated and actual results. The accountants also prepare an evaluation of all capital investment decisions two years after investments are made.

The marketing director is quite pleased with the work of the accountants—with two exceptions. First, the accountants are determined to use average costs instead of incremental costs, he says. "We can't convince accountants that negative gross margins might be profitable in the short run if idle capacity exists." The company's financial statements typically show a loss on products exported to Caribbean countries. Such products are manufactured, however, only when the company has idle capacity, so the marketing director would prefer some form of contribution reporting rather than allocating overhead on an average cost basis. The marketing director describes overhead allocations as a complete mystery.

The second criticism of accountants concerns the amount of setup costs. As mentioned earlier, the company usually makes only products that can be produced over long periods of time (at least 72 continuous hours). The marketing director repeatedly has tried to find out the extra costs involved in shorter production runs, but the stock answer is "It's too expensive." The marketing director feels that if he had a proper knowledge of costs, he sometimes could charge a price sufficiently high to permit the manufacture of low-volume products. The cost system, however, apparently is designed to allocate setup costs only over long production runs.

Summary

The Canadian Glass & Plastics Co. is somewhat unusual in that it produces consumer products, most of which are not marketed directly to the consumer. Management does view the individual consumer, however, as the ultimate customer and centers discussions of need and functionality with that in mind. The ultimate decision to make a new product rests at a rather low line level—with the product managers. This low level of responsibility is related to the relatively low capital that usually is needed.

New-product decisions seemingly are based on rather accurate accounting estimates, yet there is a great deal of marketing department criticism of the method of financial reporting used. The director of marketing feels that incremental reporting would result in better decisions—particularly with respect to utilization of idle capacity. We received the impression, however, that the company's success with new products more often has been in spite of the accounting data rather than because of the figures. On the contrary, the success ratio of individual products may be enhanced by the data received, but overall corporate profits may be hurt.

Canadian Mills, Ltd.

Until recently, Canadian Mills, Ltd. (CM Co.) was an independent corporation listed on the major Canadian stock exchanges. It has been acquired by another Canadian corporation so now is a wholly owned subsidiary. The company is primarily a processor of dry food products. Annual sales are slightly less than $100 million.

The responsibility for new-product development at CM Co. rests primarily with the marketing director. This individual's previous title was new-product director, but that title was abandoned in favor of marketing director. Reporting to the marketing director are the various product managers and the head of R&D. The marketing director reports to the division vice president (top operating officer at CM Co.).

The definition of a new product at CM Co. would include anything new other than flavor changes and new packages. The company has an extensive policy manual (titled *New-Product Development Procedural Manual*) which spells out the new-product development process, emphasizing procedures to be followed, and which includes numerous forms and exhibits. The marketing director and vice president refer to the manual quite often.

The New-Product Decision Process

The marketing director generates many ideas for new products on regular scouting trips to supermarkets in Buffalo, New York. He also conducts informal supermarket visits in other U.S. and European cities. The marketing director claims that he comes up with at least half a dozen new-product ideas every time he visits a foreign supermarket.

At least 20 ideas are generated during periodic brainstorming sessions with company sales personnel. At the end of each meeting, the sales people take a secret ballot to determine their 10 favorite ideas. The marketing director then evaluates these 10. The company admits, however, that despite these sessions it is not an innovator. All product ideas are simply copies of products already on the market in the United States or England because that is the only way for a Canadian company to survive. The Canadian market is viewed as too small to risk investing in any product that has not proved successful elsewhere.

Previously the company used contests to encourage employees to submit ideas. Although hundreds of ideas were generated under this program, none of the ideas ever culminated in a product that was introduced nationally. Consequently, the program was dropped.

When the marketing director likes an idea, he does some preliminary profit estimates in coordination with the vice president. The two then decide whether to proceed. The next step is to conduct concept interviews with consumers. Consumers are asked whether they like the idea, what advantages and disadvantages they can foresee, what price they would be willing to pay, and whether they would be willing to buy the product.

If consumers like the idea and the desired price range seems likely to offer a profit, then R&D receives the concept for purposes of developing a prototype. If R&D is successful, the product next is taken to a shopping mall where taste tests are conducted with consumers. In addition to asking shoppers how they like the taste, testers repeat questions from the initial concept interviews. Following the taste tests, the R&D lab may have to make minor revisions in the product.

The next step is to conduct in-home tests. Consumers are given packages of the product. A few days later, interviewers call them for their reactions. After the telephone interview, the company offers the respondent a reward for cooperating—either another package of the product or money equivalent to the retail value. If more than 70% select the product, the company considers the test successful.

A couple of weeks later, interviewers telephone those respondents who accepted the free package of the product and offer them the opportunity to buy the company's remaining stock at the fair retail value. Consumers who agree to make a purchase are then told, "We were just fooling you; we are going to *give* you the additional packages." Again, at least 70% have to be willing to put up their own money for the product before the marketing director will allow the product to proceed to the next stage.

Estimates of cost and volume are the next factors to be considered. Price estimates are based on what competitors charge. If the product meets contribution margin guidelines and has a payback of three years or less, then the company decides to manufacture the product. Failure to meet these financial guidelines is the primary reason most products are abandoned. We were not told what contribution margin rate the company uses in its decisions, but it is some rate higher than the division average. Therefore, if a product meets management's expectations, the average margin for the division will be improved. Alternatively, a product failing to meet expectations will not necessarily lower the average margin for the division. This methodology results in risk avoidance.

The company has never used any form of test marketing. The marketing director explained that Canada is too spread out and regionalized to make test marketing worthwhile, and test marketing could be more expensive than national failure of a product. Thus, the company prefers to take its chances without benefit of test market information. Besides, it knows that the product already is successful in another country.

Although the purchasing and production departments are not involved in the decision process, they are kept informed as to the progress of all new products through special report forms. Thus, when the marketing director is ready to begin production, there is little delay because purchasing and production have been forewarned.

Market share percentage is of some importance in the decision process because most products must have at least 5% of the market or distributors will not handle the product. The marketing director says there is no such thing as having 3% of the market. A product either has 5% or above, or it drops to zero.

The company has no other nonfinancial objectives. Idle capacity is not a consideration. The marketing director feels that the company constantly must introduce new products in order for employees to maintain their excitement about the company. Thus, no additional emphasis is placed on new products during periods of idle capacity than at any other time.

Factors such as product safety have never been a consideration although packaging sometimes is designed to avoid specific types of infestations. Neither are government regulations, ecology, or social responsibility considerations in the decision process.

Canadian Mills monitors new products for three years through regular monthly financial statements which show sales and contribution margins, along with budget estimates, by product and by region. CM Co. does not use quantitative models to assist in the new-product development process. The process is not considered complicated enough to warrant the use of such models. Even life-cycle models are not used because the marketing director does not believe in such models. Although no studies have been conducted concerning price elasticity, the marketing director thinks he has a good feel for such figures because of his experience with the company's regular products over the years.

The company does no follow-up studies to determine why products have failed after being introduced. The marketing director told us that he had made such a study once years ago, but no meaningful information resulted. He wished, however, that he had the time and resources to make more follow-up studies.

The go, no-go decisions at CM Co. are made at a number of points:

1. Following initial evaluation by the marketing director and vice president,
2. Following concept interviews with consumers,
3. Following the failure of R&D to develop a prototype,
4. Following consumer taste tests,
5. Following telephone interviews with in-home testers,
6. Following telephone conversation with in-home testers who are asked to buy the product,
7. Following calculation of contribution margin and payback.

With the exception of the first point above, the decisions are the marketing director's responsibility. Abandonment rates are quite high, and only about 3% of all ideas actually reach the prototype stage. Of those ideas making it past point 3 above, only about 10% are ever introduced nationally. Decision point 7 was cited as the major cause of abandonment of prototypes.

Assessment of Accounting Data

The marketing director and vice president were not overly complimentary with respect to the work of the company accountants.

No one is happy with the monthly financial statements. In addition, product managers regularly complain about the mismatching of advertising expense. Advertising often is paid in the month before the sales occur or in the month following the corresponding sales. There needs to be a better means of matching advertising costs to the resulting benefits.

Another criticism concerns the availability of cost accountants. Virtually all cost accounting of new products is done by the marketing director. Accountants are willing to do such work, but it always takes three weeks or more for them to work the jobs into their schedules. Cost accountants need to be assigned to marketing on a day-to-day basis. Keeping a separate accounting department causes much of the problem. The marketing director would prefer that cost accountants work for him directly and not be assigned to a separate department: "We have to penetrate the accounting department structure before getting anything done."

The marketing director also says that he receives a great variety of reports which go directly into the wastebasket. Because the accountants have a copying machine, everyone gets a copy of everything they do, regardless of whether the data are of any value.

Summary

CM Co. is another example of a Canadian company which reduces its new-product risk by imitating products already successful in the United States and England. The new-product decision process is dominated by one person—the marketing director. The decision process is based primarily on objective data such as consumer survey results. Most abandonments, however, occur because the product's contribution margin and payback do not meet company guidelines.

The new-product development process is quite organized at CM Co. The company even has a detailed policy manual outlining the steps to be followed. The abandonment percentage is quite high—particularly for a company which could be categorized as an imitator.

Chapter 4

Analysis of Interview Results

When we analyzed the new-product decision process at our 17 companies in the United States and Canada, we observed one common thread: Few similarities exist among them. We expected some degree of difference because of the large number of industries represented in the sample, but the numerous methodologies employed by these companies make it difficult to generalize about most steps in the decision process. Most of the differences can be explained, however, by the special circumstances involved in each decision process. For example, the cost of entering the market often corresponded to the organization level within the company where the responsibility for new products rested. Lower-level managers, for instance, were responsible for new products when the necessary investment was quite low. There are numerous aspects to the new-product decision process.

Definition of New Products

The definition of a new product was usually quite simple: A new product is something that the company is not manufacturing currently. In some cases this definition included new shapes and sizes of old products. Most of the companies had such broad definitions of new products that items such as color and flavor changes were included. One company's definition (Canadian Glass & Plastics) was so broad as to include existing products that were to be introduced into a new type of market. The most unusual definitions probably were held by the beer and wine producers where a new product was something that could be marketed to a segmented portion of the company's regular market. Paper Products Co. included new manufacturing processes under the definition of new products, while other companies incorporated a broad definition into some statement such as "anything which will meet currently unmet consumer needs." These same companies considered new sizes as meeting that definition.

Alternatively, other companies omitted flavor changes, new colors, and line extensions from the new-product definition. For example, R Co. included only "new things—not new sizes." Similarly, H Co. and AH Co. defined new products as something that would require a new brand name. Despite these exceptions, the typical definition of new products includes anything new to the company, even line extensions and color changes. In other words, a new product is something which is not currently being marketed by the company in question.

The Decision Makers

The individuals responsible for making the new-product decision usually were marketing oriented and located at the division level. Only one company required approval at the corporate level—at CW Co., where joint approval was required by both the corporate-level marketing manager and the division general manager (highest officer of the division). This corporate-level approval was considered necessary in order to avoid problems with more than one division producing the same product (all divisions had similar manufacturing capabilities).

Three of the companies we interviewed used committees to make decisions regarding new products. Two were Canadian. A fourth company, also in Canada, used a committee of vice presidents in the evaluation process, but only the vice president of marketing made the decision. Committees typically involved individuals with a variety of backgrounds—usually marketing, engineering, production, R&D, and finance.

Two companies told us that the decisions were made jointly by two individuals, a superior and a subordinate. Thus, it would seem more correct to categorize them as needing two levels of approval rather than as joint decisions.

As mentioned previously, with the exception of those companies using a committee structure, the new-product decision typically involved a marketing person. In only two companies did the primary new-product decisions not involve marketing. They were R Co., where the president had a general management background, and PP Co., where the division vice president had an R&D background. Paper Products Co. also was unique in that the people working on new products had a wide variety of backgrounds. The company intentionally clouded descriptions of the background necessary for a person working in the new-product department. A creative mind was considered more important than any specific type of experience or educational background.

Table 1 shows the levels at which the companies made their new-product decisions. At three of the companies, all decisions were made at the fourth level—product line manager. A fourth company (B Co.) placed the initial responsibility with the product line manager, but higher-level approvals were required in order to proceed with an idea. The instances of companies placing the new-product responsibility at this lowest level involved cases of relatively small capital investments. The reverse of this correlation, however, was not true—small investments do not always correspond to low levels of responsibility. For instance, at both R Co. and CW Co. the president was responsible for new-product decisions despite investments that could be classified as small.

Four companies had at least three levels of responsibility involved in new-product decisions although the two higher levels were required only to approve decisions to continue with a new product. The lowest-level manager could make an abandonment decision without approval from above, which meant essentially that a low-level manager had to obtain approval before investing additional funds in a project. Alternatively, no approval was necessary in order to withhold spending.

Only four companies had individuals holding some title such as "new-product manager." This information is not too meaningful, however, because people bearing other titles stated that at least 90% of their work was involved with new products. Of those persons holding a new-product manager title, two were at the third level (marketing director) and one was at the fourth level. The last individual holding a new-product manager title was a staff person at a company using a committee system. This staff person had no decision-making responsibility other than through his vote on the committee.

The presidential-level person had at least approval responsibility for new products at five companies, both small and large. The president was involved in the decision process directly at only two U.S. companies, however, and these were smaller companies in which the president had been with the organization more than 30 years. The three other presidents involved in the new-product decison process were located in Canada.

What management level *should* be involved in the new-product decision process? The president of a leading marketing research firm has noted a trend toward more presidential involvement in new-product decisions. During the 1960s, he says, "The whole mar-

TABLE 1

Levels at Which New-Product Decisons Are Made

Companies in Case Studies

	F	AF	R	H	AH	P	PT	S	PP	B	CF	CS	CFP	CW	CB	CM	CG
Committee												CS	CFP		CB**		
Top Level (President or Division Manager)			R			P	PT				CF		CFP	CW		CM	
Second Level (VP - Marketing, etc.)				H	AH		PT	S	PP		CF			CW*	CB	CM	
Third Level (Marketing Director)				H	AH				PP	B	CF		CFP				
Fourth Level (Product Line Manager)	F	AF								B							CG
New-Product Manager (with that title)					AH	P				B			CFP				

*CW's new products are approved by the head of marketing at the corporate level and the top officer of a division. This is a joint decison.

**CB's committee is strictly advisory.

keting process was fundamentally built around the concept of brand management at middle levels of corporate management. The whole thing has now come full circle to the point where brands are managed at high levels by dominant presidents."[1] The reason for this change in responsibility is attributed to the greater cost of being successful in many consumer markets. Also, the problems of introducing new products become more acute when money is tight—a situation that has existed for many companies in recent years. Consequently, those companies having a president active in the new-product decison process may be the leaders in a new management trend. Alternatively, those companies simply may be ones experiencing tight money problems.

Eight companies in our study had a vice president ultimately responsible for new products. At three of these companies, however, the vice president's role was primarily one of approving the decisions of others. Again, the size of the companies utilizing a vice president in the new-product decision process varied from the smallest in the study to the largest.

Overall there seems to be a difference in the persons responsible for making new-product decisions at Canadian and U.S. companies. We observed that Canadian companies were more common users of committees to make decisions. Also, the top operating officer was involved more often at Canadian firms. Company size differences may partially explain the differences in the role of the president, but, alternatively, the inverse of this proposition is not necessarily true. For example, F Co. and AF Co. are both relatively small furniture manufacturers, but all new-product decisions were made at the lowest level of responsibility.

That there is so much similarity among companies in the same industries leads to another possible conclusion. Perhaps there is something about the nature of an industry that leads to a given decision process. For example, the furniture companies want to introduce at least 20 new products each year in each line. Therefore, the great quantity of decisions to be made would preclude consideration at any level higher than product-line manager. Alternatively, R Co. introduces only one or two new products each year, so its president can play a major role in bringing those products to the market. Reliance on numbers, however, is not always a meaningful way of determining who might be responsible for new products. For example, PP Co. claims to work on a thousand or more new prod-

---

[1]Merrill Brown, "Marketing Expert Foresees Era of Superbrands," *Clarion-Ledger* (Jackson, Miss.), December 17, 1982, p. D-1.

ucts each year, but the decisons are made at the levels of vice president and marketing director.

Although not shown in Table 1, in most companies new-product decisions also are made by an individual in either R&D or engineering. These decisions involve abandonments because of technological impossibilities. If a prototype cannot be built or machinery cannot be designed, then the product cannot be introduced. Abandonments for these reasons are rare, however. Virtually all companies in our sample indicated that getting the R&D or engineering work completed was a mere formality. These departments might be slow sometimes, but they could do anything.

In summary, new-product decision makers vary. Some companies use committees; most use individuals. There is little similarity among companies except for those operating in the same industries. The only certainty with respect to decison makers is that they almost always have a marketing background.

New-Product Policy Manual

As shown in Table 2, only five companies had new-product policy manuals, somewhat surprising given the emphasis that most management textbooks place on them. A policy manual can serve as a reference source when no precedent for a particular action exists and can ensure adherence to stated goals and objectives. Companies with manuals generally (with one exception) had quite detailed manuals which included the variety of forms used throughout the new-product decision process.

Perhaps the best explanation of why so few companies used policy manuals relates to the fact that creativity cannot be hampered by arbitrary policies. Most companies told us that the new-products area was the only area for which a policy manual did not exist. The vice president at PP Co. said that prescribed policies are detrimental to the new-product development process because creativity can take place in a variety of environments. PP Co. does not want to risk stifling a development by forcing a creative individual to follow predetermined guidelines.

There were no identifiable similarities among the companies which had policy manuals. Both large and small companies had manuals, as did companies introducing many products and companies introducing few products per year. Our overall impression, however, is that few companies use them.

TABLE 2

Considerations in New-Product Decision Process

Companies in Case Studies

	F	AF	R	H	AH	P	PT	S	PP	B	CF	CS	CFP	CW	CB	CG	CM
Existence of Policy																	
Manual				H	AH		PT			B		CS				CG	CM
Innovator	F	AF		H	AH	P	PT	S	PP	B	CF	CS	CFP	CW	CB	CG	CM
Imitator	F	AF	R	H	AH	P	PT	S		B	CF	CS	CFP			CG	
Test Market Used				H	AH	P	PT			B	CF						
Regional Introduction Used								S	PP						CB		
Rate-of-Return Measures:																	
Payback				H	AH	P		S		B	CF	CS		CW	CB	CG	CM
Discounted Cash Flow			R	H	AH	P	PT	S	PP		CF	CS	CFP		CB	CG	
Gross Profit																	
Percentage	F	AF	R														
Contribution Margin											CF						
Percentage								S	PP			CS	CFP	CW		CG	CM
Life Cycles Used						P			PP				CFP				
Learning Curves Used						P			PP								
Sensitivity Analysis Used						P			PP			CS			CB		

Corporate and Product Objectives

The only overall corporate objectives with which any of the respondents were familiar dealt with profitability. Every manager was concerned either with a percentage return-on-investment or a return in terms of absolute dollars of income. At three companies the corporate objectives were communicated as desired gross profit percentages.

Specific product objectives often were nonexistent. Six companies reported no such objectives. Four companies, all in the United States, listed the use of regular distribution channels as a requisite every new product had to meet. A couple of companies had objectives of developing new products only in specific fields—for instance, pet products (PT Co.) and consumer foods (CFP Co.) Still another company (CF Co.) had an objective of producing only high-quality products. Although several companies implied that their new products were limited to those which could be produced with existing idle capacity, CG Co. was the only one stating it as a formal objective.

In summary, both corporate and product objectives with respect to new products are minimal. As long as a potential product appears to be profitable, there are few limitations on creativity. Apparently the lack of guidelines is considered to be more helpful than harmful.

Origin of Ideas

Companies obtain ideas for new products in a variety of ways. Imitation of others is the most common method of getting an idea. Twelve companies produced at least some new products that imitated competitors' products. To get into a market early, managers typically visited stores and trade shows in avant-garde areas. For instance, F Co. visited furniture stores in San Diego, and Canadian companies visited both U.S. and European stores. Several U.S. companies also visited Europe for ideas.

Canadian companies relied more on imitation than U.S. companies. Even though two Canadian companies produced some innovative products, all seven companies surveyed relied heavily on imitation. None of the managers to whom we spoke was ashamed of his philosophy. The typical explanation was that the small size of the Canadian market limited the amount of money that could be spent on innovative research. Consequently, it was more profitable for companies to produce products that were successful elsewhere. None of the companies producing imitative products have had patent infringement problems, however. Some respondents cited the fact that they have always made enough cosmetic changes to avoid problems, and others said that copying competitors' products was such a common practice that there was no way to police such infringements. Table 2 summarizes the innovator/imitator dichotomy. Note that six companies fall into both categories.

As to the specific person who originates new-product ideas, it is often the decision maker who generates the idea. At four Canadian and nine U.S. companies the decision maker was the primary originator of ideas. He was not, however, the sole generator of ideas at any U.S. company. At five U.S. companies (including P Co. where the committee rules), in fact, the decision maker based his ideas on concept surveys conducted with consumers.

The next most prolific source of new-product ideas was the company's sales force. Six companies used sales personnel to generate ideas. Retail store managers and customers also provided ideas to four companies. R&D departments played a major role in idea generation at only one company (PP Co.) and a minor role at three other companies. Other employees were used to generate ideas at only three companies. At two of these companies, the employees contributing successful ideas were rewarded for their efforts.

Individuals outside the corporation and its distribution channels occasionally have played minor roles in the generation of new-product ideas. Only two companies—both sporting goods manufacturers—reported using ideas contributed by consumers. The U.S. company paid for the ideas used; the Canadian manufacturer did not. The same two companies also reported receiving usable ideas from other outsiders, specifically suppliers of raw materials and managers at sister subsidiaries. Table 3 summarizes each company's sources of new-product ideas.

As can be observed in Table 3, the creation of new-product ideas usually is the responsibility of only one individual within an organization. Although sales personnel sometimes play a minimal role in the development of ideas, other employees' contributions are negligible. More often than not, the decision maker must generate his own new-product ideas and then follow through to abandonment or introduction.

TABLE 3

Persons Contributing New-Product Ideas

Companies in Case Studies

Decision Maker (aided by surveys)	H				B						CM
Decision Maker (unaided)	F	AF	R			CF	CFP	CW		CG	CM
Sales Personnel	F	AF	R						CB	CG	
R & D			P	S	PP	CS					
Other Employees			P	S	B					CG	
Are Employees Rewarded?			Yes (P)		Yes (B)					No (CG)	
Customers				S		CS					
Suppliers and Others				S		CS					

Role of R&D

As mentioned earlier, R&D does not play a major role in the conception of new products. At only one company (PP Co.), which considered itself technology oriented, did R&D play the major role at the idea stage. R&D usually is viewed as a service department which builds new products to meet specifications supplied by someone in marketing.

Surprisingly, there was little criticism of the R&D function. Interviewees said that ideas are turned over to the R&D department and within a few weeks, almost by magic, the new-product prototype is invented. In some cases, R&D later revises a prototype because consumers have recommended additional features. Overall, R&D plays a minor role in the new-product decision process but only because the R&D employees are so good at their jobs. It is only when the R&D department is unsuccessful that the new-product decision process is influenced noticeably.

Criteria Used for Evaluation

A variety of criteria are used to evaluate new products depending upon the stage in the development process. Initially an idea or concept has to offer the potential for success. In some companies this evaluation is a subjective one based on the opinion of the person responsible for new products. At other companies the initial evaluation is based on consumer surveys. These latter companies typically base their decisions on whether consumers *need* the new product, while the former companies base their decisions on whether consumers are apt to *buy* the new item. The difference in objectives is probably more philosophical than real.

Before some companies develop a prototype (for example, H Co. and P Co.) they evaluate the idea in conjunction with government regulations and the company's social responsibility. These are major factors in some industries but practically disregarded in others, depending upon the nature of the companies' products and the type of raw materials used.

Once an idea has been developed into a prototype, the next step is to evaluate the aesthetics or taste (or both) of the new item. This decision may be made in-house, or the company may send the product to tasting labs or actual consumers. Sometimes sales personnel or distributors are substituted for consumers. One company (S. Co.) includes its advertising agency as a key evaluator at this stage of the process.

If the prototype is attractive and tasteful, the next step is to calculate return-on-investment figures or to test market the product. Obviously those companies not using test markets will prepare ROI figures as the next step. Some companies that do use test markets, however, also prepare ROI estimates prior to test marketing. The test market results then are compared to the predetermined figures.

Seven of the companies we interviewed have formal test marketing programs. Three additional companies introduce new products on a regional basis and thus obtain some of the benefits of test marketing. Four of the seven companies which do not use test marketing are located in Canada. Respondents at these companies explained that test marketing was not necessary because their products were similar to products already successful in the United States. The three U.S. companies using neither test markets nor regional introductions were companies which did not have to invest in inventories. They used trade shows to introduce new products, so only a prototype was necessary to generate sales orders. Their low cost of getting a new product onto the market did not warrant an investment in test marketing.

The manager at one company (S Co.) which occasionally uses regional introductions explained that test markets are not used because the company is fearful that a trade association might pass a rule against the new product before a sufficient number get into the hands of consumers. Still another company (H Co.) uses a laboratory test market whenever secrecy is of the essence. Table 2 summarizes the test marketing practices of each company surveyed.

By itself, test marketing is not really a criterion for evaluating new products. Instead, test markets are used to obtain data necessary to compute ROI statistics. Such factors as profit margins and market size are estimated based on the test market results.

The specific criteria used to evaluate new-product decisions include discounted cash flow analysis, payback, gross profit percentage, and contribution margin percentage. The last statistic —contribution margin percentage—is used only in Canada. Table 2 also summarizes the various financial measures used in the evaluation of new products.

Twelve companies use discounted cash flow analysis. This method is accompanied by the use of the payback method at eight companies. Thus, new products must offer not only a high rate of return but also a short payback period. Because of the risk involved in new products, companies like to get their money back in a hurry in case consumer tastes change. One manager mentioned that payback intentionally was not used because the company (CFP Co.) was more concerned with long-term growth than with short-term profits.

116

Gross profit margins are used at most Canadian companies and at those U.S. companies where decisions are made at a relatively low managerial level. All U.S. companies which use gross profit margin as a criterion are instances of either low initial investment or cases where the new product is quite similar to existing products (B Co.).

At two Canadian companies contribution margin percentage is used to evaluate new-product ideas. In addition, managers at other Canadian companies lamented that this methodology is not being used in their organizations. It seems as though the concepts of incremental costing and contribution reporting are much better known by marketing executives in Canada than in the United States.

At one Canadian company not using contribution reporting, a marketing executive commented that it is necessary to ignore the accountants' reports when making new-product decisions during times of idle capacity. Everyone in marketing and production understands that even though estimates based on average costs show a new product to be a loser, the total profits of a department will increase. Although ignoring the accountants' estimates is preferable to utilizing the average cost figures, the managers do not always have the full information necessary to make the most accurate decision.

Importance of Market Share Size

Managers at almost every company told us that market share percentage has some impact on new-product decisions. The general consensus was that a company must gain a certain market share for a new product to be successful, regardless of what the return-on-investment statistics show, because members of the distribution channel will not handle a product if volume is not sufficient to garner at least a minimal share of the market. For example, several companies stated that there is no such thing as a product having 3% of a market. If a product does not have at least a 5% share, distributors will stop carrying the item—thus reducing the market share to zero. Consequently, if test marketing shows a new product to be extremely profitable with a 3% market share, the item will be abandoned because there is no such thing as a 3% share in some markets. Actually, 11 companies emphasized the importance of market share to their distributors.

Other companies consider market share in terms of absolute volume of sales rather than as a percentage of the market. For

117

instance, the furniture companies want to produce at least 500 units at a time, and CG Co. wants at least three days of production at a time. Companies have these volume criteria because of the high setup costs associated with a production run. Rather than compute the setup costs for every specific product, the company follows an established rule that associates sales volume with profitability.

One company (CFP Co.) took the market share criterion to the extreme in that it will produce a product only if the company can be number one in the market. The explanation for this philosophy is that a large market share is necessary to warrant the advertising expenditures needed to entice large Canadian chain stores to carry the product.

In summary, market share percentage is a major criterion in the new-product decision process. In fact, only two companies (PP Co. and CB Co.) stated that market share was unimportant if the financial objectives were met. Although the reasons for having a market share criterion differed among companies, the predominant reason for such a policy was because of the influence of distributors on a new product's success.

Nonfinancial Criteria

As shown in Table 4, a variety of nonfinacial criteria often are considered in the new-product decision process. Product safety is a major consideration at five companies: the two manufacturers of sporting goods and the three makers of large consumer products. In most cases the companies cited their concern for product safety to be associated with previous liability suits that had made management more cautious. None of the manufacturers of food or beverages consider product safety, but surely it is an underlying assumption for such products.

Considerations of ecology and the environment play a role in the decision process at only four companies—two in the United States and two in Canada—and they have manufacturing processes that cause smelly emissions. Considerations dealing with environmental protection were attributable to companies' desire to be good corporate citizens rather than because of the existence of any antipollution laws.

Ten of the companies we surveyed reported that government or industry group regulations have to be considered when they develop new products. The regulations typically do not result in the

TABLE 4
Nonfinancial Criteria in New-Product Decisions

Companies in Case Studies

	F	AF	R	H	AH	P	PT	S	PP	B	CF	CS	CFP	CW	CB	CG	CM
Market Share Percentage	F	AF	R	H	AH	P	PT	S		B	CF	CS	CFP	CW		CG	CM
Product Safety	F	AF	R					S				CS			CB	CG	
Ecology						P			PP						CB	CG	
Government or Industry Regulations	F	AF	R	H	AH	P		S			CF	CS				CG	
Blocking a Competitor or Round out a Line	F	AF	R	H	AH	P		S			CF	CS	CFP			CG	
Social Responsibility				H					PP		CF	CS	CFP			CG	
Idle Capacity								S	PP	B		CS	CFP	CW	CB	CG	
"Gut Feelings" Important			R				PT										

119

abandonment of new products. Instead, products sometimes have to be reworked to meet regulatory requirements.

The nature of the regulations varies from one company to the next. Two companies consider the requirements of industry trade groups limiting factors. The two furniture manufacturers must be concerned with special raw materials required in products that are to be shipped into California. Those companies which manufacture medicines have to consider federal regulations restricting the quantity of certain chemicals that go into consumer products. Overall, government and industry regulations play only a minor role in the new-product decision process, but it seems greater in the United States than in Canada.

Managements at seven companies stated that they would go into production with a new product despite marginal estimates of profitability if the product would fill a niche in the product line or would block a competitor out of a market. Indirectly this is a financial objective because the new product is expected to contribute to overall profits or to future profits. In some cases, such as at S Co., which sometimes produces unprofitable sporting equipment for children, these new products are considered investments for the future.

Eight companies—four in the United States and four in Canada—cited corporate social responsibility as a new-product decision criterion. At most companies, social responsibility seemingly played a very minor role. Management probably talked about social responsibility only because it sounded as if it would make good public relations. At least one company, however, does give strong consideration to social responsibility during the new-product decision process. H Co. management stated that many ideas had been abandoned because they failed to meet the company's social goals.

H Co.'s management also gave us examples of new-product ideas which had been abandoned even though the company had the technology to produce the items and the profit expectations looked good. Management, however, felt that it would be unethical to market these items even though there were no laws prohibiting sale. Indeed, social responsibility is an important criterion in the new-product decison process at H Co.

Table 4 includes the aspect of existing idle capacity as a nonfinancial criterion, which is probably improper given that the existence of idle capacity results in less need for capital investment. Consequently, idle capacity is actually a financial criterion—but only indirectly at most companies. Only eight companies cited the existence of idle capacity as an important factor, and five of these are in Canada.

Idle capacity is called a nonfinancial criterion because the decision maker is not given a choice of acquiring new facilities or utilizing idle capacity. New products can be introduced at these companies only when idle capacity exists. Thus, idle capacity must be available before the decision can be made to proceed with a new product. In some cases, new products are limited to those which can be produced in a specific factory, on a specific machine, or at a specific time of year.

Another reason for calling idle capacity a nonfinancial criterion is the manner in which costs are computed on new products. New-product cost estimates invariably are assigned full allocations of overhead. Thus, the decision maker often has no financial incentive to utilize idle capacity.

One additional nonfinancial criterion is "gut feelings." This factor was noted at two companies (R Co. and PT Co.). In both cases, the president had a voice in the decision process, and it was his "gut feelings" that resulted in products being introduced despite objective evidence that would warrant a different decision. Given that both instances of "gut feelings" involved a top corporate official, and these were the only two U. S. companies in which the president was involved in the decision process, we hypothesize that "gut feelings" may be a more important criterion at companies where the top officer is involved in the decision process—namely at small companies.

In summary, nonfinancial criteria play at least a small role at every company we surveyed. Some companies, as shown in Table 4, have as many as four or five criteria which new products must meet. Rarely, however, do any of these criteria result in abandonments. Instead, prototypes are reworked until they meet the established guidelines.

Budget Constraints

We were surprised that budget constraints rarely play a role in the new-product decision process. Only three companies (PP Co., B Co., and CFP Co.) cited budget constraints as a limiting factor. At these three companies, budget constraints apparently were a real problem judging from the amount of management complaining. None of the executives at the other companies surveyed even implied that there were any informal budget constraints.

Generally, the reason given for the lack of budget constraints was the overall importance of new products to a company's continuing success. One manager stated that he had a budget, but this was no constraint because budgets could be revised for any good reason, and the best possible reason to revise a budget was a new product which had the potential to enhance profits.

At some companies, budgets were communicated in such a way that managers were evaluated on the basis of a specified gross profit margin. This setup is not really a budget constraint because the manager can spend an unlimited amount on new products as long as the products reach the desired profit margin.

Pricing Strategies

Many of the companies surveyed use quite unsophisticated pricing strategies. Only five companies—all in the United States—use test markets to estimate price elasticity. Three additional companies—two of them Canadian—conduct surveys of company salespeople to determine opinions regarding price elasticity. The nine remaining companies do not analyze price strategies. These nine base their prices to some extent on what competitors are charging. Four companies actually set prices before they create the product. For example, furniture companies would attempt to invent a chair that would sell for $300. Subsequently, if the finished product did not offer a profit at that price, the product would be abandoned. It seemed there was no way the price could be increased. These price points were, however, set arbitrarily and were based upon the "gut feelings" of the decision maker.

Four other companies charge prices the same as competitors or slightly lower. Only one company bases its prices strictly on cost without regard to the actions of competitors.

Pricing seems to be one of the more unsophisticated aspects of the new-product decision process. Even those companies which use multiple test markets to evaluate pricing alternatives use only two. Usually managers establish prices based on their personal feelings as to what the market will bear. Table 5 summarizes the pricing strategies of the various companies.

Use of Quantitative Tools and Follow-up Studies

Fewer than half the companies in the study use what might be called sophisticated quantitative tools in their new-product decision process or do any follow-up studies of why products fail. Manage-

TABLE 5
Pricing Strategies

Companies in Case Studies

Pricing Strategy	Companies
Based on Test Market Studies	H AH P PT R
Based on Opinion Surveys	B
Aim for a Price Point	F AF PP S CS CF CB
Based on Competitors' Prices	CG
Markup on Cost	CFP CW CM

ment at those companies which do use quantitative tools, however, were quite enthusiastic about the results generated. Table 2 shows the companies which in some way use life cycle models, learning curves, and sensitivity analysis during the new-product decision process. Both P Co. and PP Co. use all three types of tools. Four companies use life cycle models, four use sensitivity analysis, and three build the use of learning curves into the decision process. Managers at other companies indicated that they sometimes use the critical path method in production departments to get new products into regular production. Two companies even use computer simulation models.

Companies rarely conduct follow-up studies as to why products have failed. Only four companies (P Co., PT Co., CS Co. and CFP Co.) regularly perform such studies. Managers at these companies feel they have invested so much in the new products that they want to learn the reason for failure in order to avoid future mistakes. At one company, this is even an ongoing process as semiannual reports are prepared for all new products not meeting budget expectations. More commonly, however, no studies are performed. Management does not feel it has the resources to invest additional funds to study products which are already "lost causes."

Length and Means of Monitoring Introductions

The majority of the companies we surveyed monitor the progress of newly introduced products by means of regular internal financial reports that are prepared for all products. In some cases this monitoring is handled by the individual responsible for making new-product decisions. At other companies, the new products receive no special consideration, but progress is monitored in the same manner as for existing products.

Only two companies prepare any special reports to monitor new products after they have been introduced. In one case, these special reports consist of weekly sales figures submitted by sales personnel. In the other case, product line statements showing actual versus budgeted figures are prepared only for new products. In all other companies, the monitoring of new products is based upon the regular monthly reports prepared for all products showing sales and profits by product. Product line figures then are subdivided by geographic region.

All companies, except for the two household product manufacturers, rely on accounting department reports to monitor new products. These household products companies use independent reports of retail sales prepared by the A. C. Nielsen Co. to monitor old products as well as new.

Companies located in the United States typically (with one exception) monitor new products along with existing product lines. In other words, there is no special treatment of new products once they are introduced nationally. In Canada, however, the monitoring of new products typically stays with the new-product decision maker for a period of time after introduction. Only one Canadian company (CW Co.) treats the monitoring of new products in the same manner as that of old products.

As to the length of time new products receive special monitoring after an introduction, it varies from one to three years. The six Canadian companies with special monitoring programs state the monitoring period in terms of years, as shown below:

CF Co., one year
CS Co., two years
CFP Co., one year
CB Co., one year
CG Co., one year
CM Co., three years

The single U. S. company with a special tracking program (PP Co.) monitors new products until they reach the beginning of the maturity stage of the product life cycle. This period may vary from under one year to several years.

In summary, companies located in the United States typically utilize regular monthly financial reports to monitor the progress of new products. This monitoring is the same as for existing products and is performed by the person responsible for a particular line of products. In Canada, the responsibility for monitoring an introduction stays with the new-product decision maker for a substantial period of time.

Advertising and Packaging

We grouped the subjects of advertising and packaging together because they seem to play little importance in the new-product decision process. Packaging is looked upon as a necessary evil and apparently is outside the duties of the new-product decision maker at most companies. The impression was given that packaging requirements are turned over to designers and the company uses whatever the designers want. Only at CW Co. is packaging considered a major facet of the new-product decision process. Management at CW Co. said that the label on a wine bottle plays a significant role in the success of a new product, and it must identify the personality of the bottle's contents. Consequently, the introduction of a new wine often is delayed while designers work on a label.

Advertising typically is used both in the test marketing of a new product and at the time of introduction. The responsibility for advertising usually rests with an outside advertising agency, so the person responsible for new products does not have to be concerned with the role of advertising.

Two companies consider advertising a significant factor in the development of a new product. At S Co., the advertising agency must be able to develop a believable advertising program for new sporting equipment before the company decides to develop the product. B Co. is similar in that believable, macho advertising has to be developed prior to product introduction. At other companies, the diversity of new-product offerings may make it impossible to generalize about the importance of advertising. Consequently, the new-product decision maker relinquishes the responsibility for advertising to an outside agency.

Assessment of Accounting Data

The assessment of accounting data varies tremendously among the companies we studied. In some cases, the decision maker receives little information besides cost estimates, and that is all that is desired. At other companies, the accountants serve as the hub of the new-product decision process and utilize sophisticated computer models to prepare untold reams of data. Typically, accountants provide cost estimates, ROI data, and payback figures. After a new product is introduced, financial statements, subdivided by geographic region, are prepared on the basis of individual products. Regardless of the amount of data received, most marketing executives are pleased with the work of the accountants. Executives in the United States offered few ideas as to additional services accountants could provide. This failure to offer suggestions probably is attributable to a lack of knowledge as to what accountants can do. Canadian marketing executives, however, seemed to be more accounting oriented and were able to offer suggestions more often.

At only one U. S. company did a new-product decision maker have any complaints about accounting data. This individual stated that labor cost estimates often are incorrect—thus leading to unprofitable products. The other criticism dealt with the closing date of the fiscal year. Most costs for new products are incurred late in the calendar year, but sales of new products are not recorded until at least January. Therefore, the company's December 31 closing resulted in a mismatching of expenses and revenues. The marketing executive recommends switching to a natural business year.

Accountants at U. S. companies received so little criticism for several reasons. First, marketing executives seem to have little knowledge of accounting or appreciation for how accounting data can be used. At three companies, marketing executives are given very little accounting data. At other companies, marketing executives are inundated with accounting data. In some cases, executives pay little attention to accounting data, while in others, the work of the accountants is viewed as gospel and there is full reliance thereon, without consideration of the implications of such data. In either case, the decision maker was pleased with the output received from the accounting department.

Canadian marketers seem more sophisticated with respect to their knowledge of accounting. In fact, at every Canadian company, recommendations were made by management as to how accountants can change their policies and aid the new-product decision process. These recommendations are summarized as follows:

1. Incremental costing should be used to evaluate new-product decisions.
2. Accountants should prepare fewer numbers and offer more analysis of data.
3. Accountants should be more cooperative.
4. Accountants should provide data more quickly.
5. Cost estimates should be presented as a range rather than as absolute figures.
6. Advertising costs should be properly matched to sales.
7. Accountants' reports should be meaningful to intended users.

The suggestion that incremental costing be used to evaluate new products was the most common suggestion. At two companies, marketing executives understand the benefits of incremental costing. Both of these executives commented that they repeatedly have urged accountants to change their reports, but the accountants will not change. Two other Canadian companies do use incremental costing to evaluate new product decisions. Thus, the concept of incremental costing seems to be better known among Canadian marketers than among their counterparts in the United States.

The second suggestion on the preceding list is that accountants need to provide more data analysis. Accountants were described as number crunchers, and marketers need more information based on sensitivity analysis. Comparisons to industry norms and corporate objectives also would be quite useful.

At least four companies indicated that the accounting department is generally uncooperative with respect to providing the data necessary to make new-product decisions. This lack of cooperation often is evidenced by long delays in providing requested data. In one case, the manager said the accountants are "too busy" to prepare necessary data. At another company, the structure of the accounting department is at fault. The individual who complained said it would be preferable for cost accountants to be employed under the direct supervision of the new-product decision maker instead of being isolated in a separate department. He thought the accounting supervisor was merely trying to build an empire rather than trying to supply needed services.

At still another company, the accountants failed to answer the questions asked by the marketing executive. Instead of supplying the requested cost data, the accountants cut off all discussion, saying a project was too expensive without ever supplying the requested cost data.

As a corollary to the complaint about uncooperativeness, some managers complained about the slowness with which data are provided. The accountants seem cooperative enough, but it takes weeks to get the needed data. The validity of this complaint, of course, cannot be determined without knowing what is asked of the accountants. It is reasonable to assume that the accountants sometimes dawdle prior to beginning a new-products project. Alternatively, there probably are instances when the project is so complex that the extra time is necessary to do a thorough job.

One worthwhile recommendation a marketing manager made dealt with the accountants' cost estimates. Accountants at most companies provide marketing managers with an estimate of what manufacturing costs will be for a new product. These estimates then are used to evaluate whether to proceed with or abandon a new product. The cost estimates, however, usually are based on the production of a single prototype and are subject to sizable error. Marketing managers, unfortunately, view the cost estimates as precise, so products are abandoned if they fail to meet a prescribed return-on-investment goal by even a fraction of a percent. Alternatively, work proceeds on a project which seems to meet the profitability goal. In either case, the decision may be incorrect because of erroneous cost estimates. Many examples could be given of products being introduced nationally only to be abandoned later because of excessive costs, which naturally leads to the conclusion that some prototypes probably have been abandoned when they perhaps should not have been. The marketing executive who made this observation admitted that the accountants are not at fault. The accountants make their best estimate, but they recognize that there is a great deal of imprecision involved. Marketing managers, however, assume that the cost estimates are exact. Consequently, marketing managers need to know how to use the cost estimates. The manager making this recommendation said the best way to educate the users of the data is to provide cost estimates in terms of a range rather than precise amounts. As it now stands, marketing managers often place the burden for new-product failure on the accountant. However, had the accountant been the decision maker, he or she might have recognized the impreciseness of the cost estimates and made a different decision. The presenting of cost estimates as a range of figures would not necessarily simplify the new-product decision, but at least marketing managers would be making the decision with the benefit of full information.

Another complaint we received was that advertising costs are sometimes not matched to the benefits they are expected to produce. Advertising expense sometimes is recorded at the time an advertisement appears. Sales that are the result of those advertisements, however, may not be recorded until subsequent periods. There was criticism that accountants are reluctant to consider the view that advertising is an investment in the future and treat such costs as period costs without any attempt at matching. Treating advertising as a period cost may have merit when the advertising is for established products. After all, over a period of years, any advantages of allocating advertising costs to the periods benefiting from such costs would be minimal as recurring programs would tend to produce similar results over the years. New products, however, have no benefit of previous years' advertising. Thus, a manager willing to risk the introduction of a new product should not have to currently bear the burden of immediate advertising that is expected to produce sales in subsequent periods. Consequently, capitalization of advertising costs might induce marketing managers to invest more in new products expected to produce long-term results.

The final criticism of accountants was that they provide too many unneeded reports. Since the invention of the copying machine, accountants have been providing copies of reports to people who do not need them, which results not only in the waste of paper but a danger that desired information may be thrown away along with unwanted data. Consequently, accountants should be more selective in distributing reports and send them to only those individuals who can use the reports productively.

In summary, marketing managers in the United States seem unsophisticated in their knowledge of accounting and their use of accounting data. Some managers receive little accounting data or ignore what they do receive. Others rely on a single figure without analyzing what the figure really means or how it has been calculated. Canadian marketing managers, on the other hand, seem to have a better appreciation of accountants and the information they can provide. The major areas of complaint concerning accounting data relate to the failure to use incremental costing, the mismatching of advertising expense, the need for accountants to perform more analysis work, and the general uncooperativeness or slowness of accountants.

Other than these criticisms, the only comment that can be made with regard to accountants' input into the new-product decision process is that the quantity of input varies tremendously from one company to another. In some companies, the accountants provide nothing more than some cost estimates and routine financial statements. At other companies, the accounting department is at the hub of the new-product decision process.

Chapter 5
Summary, Conclusions and Recommendations

The new-product decision process varies considerably among the companies included in our study. Naturally, such variety makes it difficult to generalize about the process. This situation, of course, is not unique to the new-product decision process. All decision processes vary from one company to the next because of differences in cognitive style among decision makers.

Cognitive styles vary from the quite systematic or analytic to the strictly intuitive. Combinations of these two extremes also are quite common. The decision maker using an analytic cognitive style relies heavily upon organized information, has a planned approach to a solution, and uses formal, rational analysis. That type of individual is illustrated best in this study by the decision maker at those companies using sophisticated computer models to arrive at an answer in evaluating a new product. Those companies relying on an analytic cognitive style reduce the problem situation to a set of underlying causal functions.

Alternatively, the intuitive decision maker lets the situation guide the decision making. The intuitive decision maker essentially learns more by acting than by analyzing. Trial and error is a prevalent tactic, and this person considers common sense more important than analytic forecasts. The intuitive style is, of course, best typified in this study by the person who relies on "gut feelings" to judge the potential success of a new product.

In between the two extremes are those individuals who are basically analytic but who rely to some extent on intuition for a certain aspect of the decision process. For example, many of the new-product decision makers are quite analytic, but the quantitative models they use are based on intuition regarding what price should be charged. Similarly, the decision maker usually evaluates the aesthetics rather than sending out a prototype for consumer panels to evaluate.

The level of uncertainty avoidance used by managers also plays a role in the decision process. New-product managers operate in such uncertain environments that they often desire to avoid risk and uncertainty at the expense of expected value. This feeling is most evident in the product imitation philosophy of some U.S. companies and most Canadian companies in the study.

Other methods of uncertainty avoidance include the reliance on fast payback and the ignoring of price elasticity studies in favor of price points common to an industry. Reliance on the payback method reduces the need to be concerned about future uncertainty. In effect, the short feedback cycle allows for frequent new decisions without having to be concerned with the greater risks associated with long-term decisions.

The emphasis on meeting price points is an example of a negotiated environment. Organizations seek to control their environment and the associated risks by adopting industry-wide conventional practices. This practice is probably just as restrictive as price fixing, and it is certainly as effective in reducing risk.

Despite the variations in management style and the many levels of risk avoidance, it still is possible to generate an overall summary of the new-product decision process as it exists at most companies—but not at all of them. The flowchart shown in Figure 5 depicts this process. It is similar to the normative flowchart shown in Chapter 2 as Figure 1.

Summary of the New-Product Decision Process

Figure 5 portrays the new-product decision process as it exists at the majority of companies participating in this study. A number of alternative paths are included in the flowchart to take into consideration alternative options that are available to new-product decision makers. For example, at step 25 in Figure 5, the question is asked whether a test market is to be used. The existence of this question makes the flowchart applicable both to companies using test marketing and those which do not. Other similar alternatives also are provided in the flowchart.

Summarizing the Flowchart

New-product decision makers initially consider corporate objectives. Typically, they know only one corporate objective—return on investment. Step 2 involves consideration of which product fields

FIGURE 5
Flowchart Depicting New-Product Decision Process

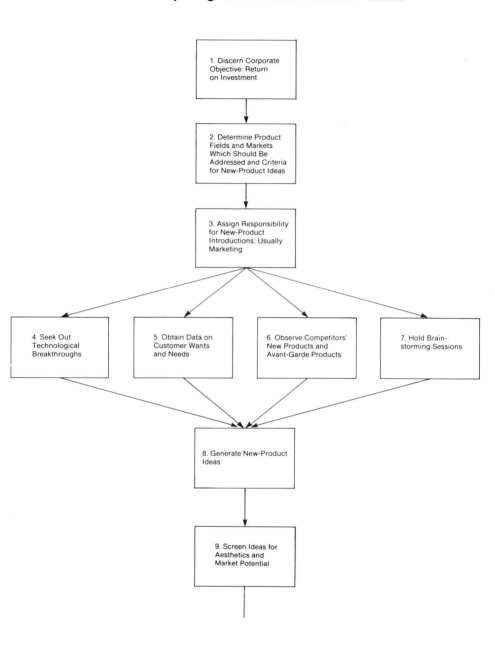

133

FIGURE 5 (Continued)

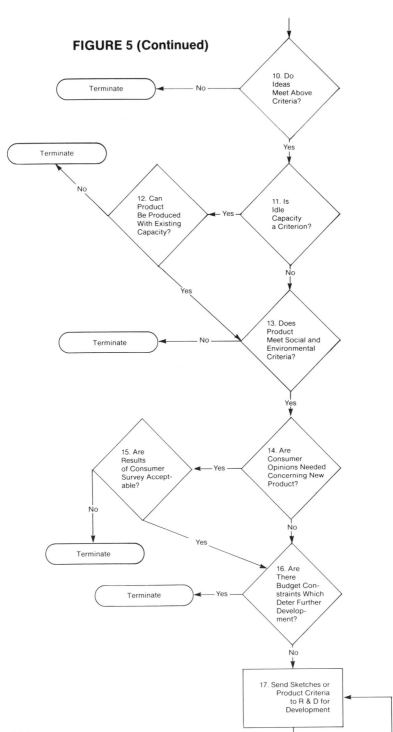

FIGURE 5 (Continued)

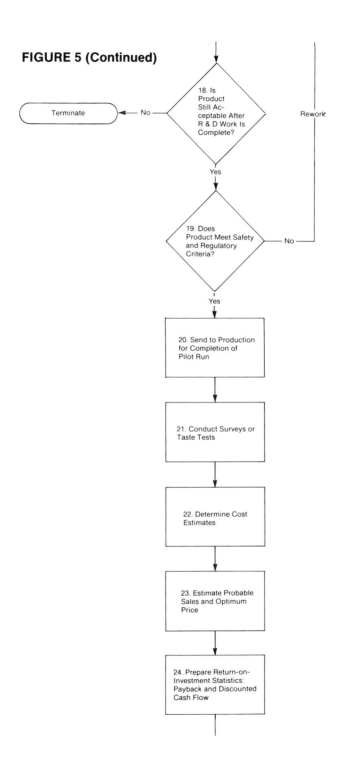

FIGURE 5 (Continued)

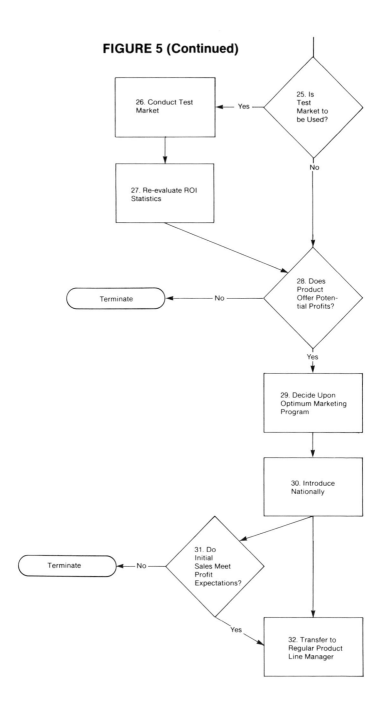

and markets should be addressed. As was true of overall corporate objectives, these product objectives are limited. Some companies have no such objectives, while others are concerned only with the distribution channels in which new products will be sold.

Step 3 requires the assignment of responsibility for new products. Usually an individual with a marketing background is given the duties of overseeing the new-product development process. This individual typically is a line manager at any one of four management levels. In a few cases, committees have been given the responsibility for new products.

Step 3 in the decision process is followed by either step 4, 5, 6, or 7. Some companies gain inspiration for new-product ideas by seeking technological breakthroughs; others conduct consumer surveys to determine customer wants and needs; still others monitor competitors' new products; and some hold brainstorming sessions with salespeople or other employees. These four different methodologies generally do not overlap. A company will use one or another of the methods but not all four.

Once inspiration has been achieved, the company moves to step 8—generating specific new-product ideas. Someone, usually the decision maker, carefully studies these ideas to determine aesthetic appeal and profit potential (step 9). Terminations occur (step 10) if ideas do not meet these criteria in the subjective opinion of the decision maker.

In step 11 the company asks whether the existence of idle capacity is to be a criterion in the decision process. If the answer is yes, step 12 asks whether the product idea can be produced with existing capacity. If the product cannot be produced with existing facilities, the project is terminated. If idle capacity is not a criterion, or if an idea meets the criterion, the next step (13) is to determine whether the product idea will meet the company's social and environmental criteria.

Step 14, although not used by all companies, involves obtaining consumers' opinions about the product idea. Following this survey, a decision (step 15) is made whether to proceed to the R & D stage. Rarely, but sometimes, there is a consideration between steps 15 and 17 involving budget constraints.

Step 17 involves the invention or development of a new product by an R & D or engineering department, which is followed in step 18 by an evaluation of whether R & D has produced the product that was requested and whether goals of aesthetics and taste are still met. If not, the product is abandoned at this step.

When a prototype does meet the desired criteria given to R & D, the next question (step 19) is whether the product is safe for consumer use and meets all government and industry regulations. Failure to meet these criteria usually is not a limiting factor. Instead, a product not meeting safety or regulatory requirements is returned to R&D for reworking.

In step 20, a regular production department is geared up for a pilot run. Step 21 involves taste tests or consumer surveys. At the same time, formal estimates of cost are prepared (step 22). Estimates also are made of probable sales and optimum selling price (step 23). All these estimates are then used (in step 24) to compute return-on-investment statistics. Discounted cash flows and payback, usually in combination, are the methods used most often. The next step (25) involves the question of whether a test market is to be used. If so, the test marketing of the new product is conducted (step 26), return-on-investment statistics are re-evaluated on the basis of test market results (step 27), and the decision is made whether to proceed to a national introduction (step 28).

The optimum marketing program is decided at step 29. If a test market was used, the marketing program is usually identical to the one used during the test market period.

After the product is introduced nationally (step 30), the responsibility for new products usually is transferred to a regular product line manager who monitors the progress of both new and old products by means of regular product-line financial statements (step 32). Alternatively, at some companies, particularly in Canada, there is a step 31 in which the new-product decision maker monitors the new product for a period of time before it is turned over to a product line manager. At such companies there is an additional opportunity to terminate a product if initial sales goals are not met.

In summary, the go, no-go decisions in the new-product decision process usually occur at the following points (the asterisks by a number indicate a point not typical at most companies):

1. Following the initial screening of the aesthetics and market potential of a new-product idea,
2. Following an evaluation of an idle capacity criterion,
3. Following evaluation of social and environmental criteria,
*4. Following evaluation of consumer opinions about a new-product idea,
*5. Following consideration of budget constraints,
6. Following development (or lack thereof) of a prototype by R&D,

7. Following evaluation of return-on-investment statistics,
*8. During introduction stage of life cycle.

With respect to abandonment rates, points 1 and 7 above are usually the most significant. In reality, point 2 sometimes is combined with point 1 and is considered part of the initial evaluation. Point 3 (social and environmental criteria) is probably the least significant factor leading to abandonment. Most managers gave "lip service" to point 3 but few could give concrete examples. Point 5 similarly is a minor consideration at most companies although three companies did rate budget constraints as an important factor. Point 8 also is a factor at only a few companies. We also should note that point 7 is quite a complex undertaking. Costs have to be estimated, and test market data or other revenue estimates must be available. All these data may be incorporated into models utilizing sensitivity and risk analysis.

Recommendations

A number of recommendations can be made based on the results of this study. Some are major and some are minor. Some might benefit certain companies but not others. However, we hope that some readers of this report will find the suggestions helpful.

Accounting Education for Marketing Managers

Marketing managers, particularly those in the United States, appear to have little knowledge of or appreciation for accounting and accountants. Perhaps marketers could make more informed decisions about new products if they had a better understanding of accounting data.

One solution to this problem might be for companies to provide accounting instruction to marketers. The accounting staff could provide detailed orientation programs for new-product decision makers. Alternatively, a better idea might be for accounting organizations such as the National Association of Accountants and the Society of Management Accountants of Canada to offer continuing education programs for marketing executives. Such programs could be offered in cooperation with a professional marketing group such as the American Marketing Association. Probably NAA and SMAC already have continuing education programs that could be easily adapted for presentation to marketing managers.

The quantity and quality of accounting data used in the new-product decision process vary tremendously from one company to the next. Consequently, all decision makers cannot be operating with full information. Educational programs, perhaps designed both for marketers and their accountants, might help improve the new-product decision process. NAA, SMAC, and the AMA are the obvious groups to provide the necessary education.

Incremental Costing

Incremental costing is a concept that deserves more study both by marketers and by accountants who serve marketing executives. When companies have excess idle capacity, it seems plausible that incremental costing might be a logical tool for them to use when computing new-product costs.

The general absence of contribution reporting came as somewhat of a surprise to us given the emphasis placed on the subject in accounting textbooks and journal articles. Also surprising was the fact that contribution reporting is used to some extent in Canada but not among U. S. new-product decision makers. Further studies should be designed to determine the effectiveness of contribution reporting and incremental costing in making new-product-related decisions.

Allocation of New-Product Development Costs

Costs of developing new products unanimously are written off as overhead. There is no attempt to match development costs to the actual products subsequently produced. Thus, a new product, once introduced to the market, is not forced to bear any of the costs incurred prior to introduction.

The matching principle supposedly is a critical factor in accounting, but that principle usually is violated when companies account for new-product development costs. The costs of developing a new product are universally written off as overhead during the period in which the costs are incurred even though the benefits which accrue because of those expenditures may not materialize until future accounting periods. This situation means that a manager is penalized in the current period for developing products that might produce long-term benefits. Alternatively, managers who invest

140

very little in new-product development will appear better in the short run. Consequently, the present accounting treatment of new-product development costs could lead to less than optimum decisions among marketing managers.

Allocation of Advertising Costs

One of the interviewees in this study mentioned the problem caused by advertising expenditures being matched improperly with the revenues resulting from the advertisements. The expense of advertising new products is recorded when the advertisements appear. The sales benefits resulting from these ads, however, may not be recorded until subsequent accounting periods. As is true of new-product development costs, the immediate expensing of advertising costs may not result in decisions that lead to a company's long-term best interests. The firm's goals are apt to become subrogated to the individual manager's personal goals for immediate success.

Even the American Accounting Association has mentioned the possibility of capitalization and subsequent amortization of advertising costs. In 1966 the Committee to Prepare a Statement of Basic Accounting Theory mentioned the possibility of recognizing future advertising benefits as an asset:

> Relevance demands that the best available techniques for allocating these expenditures to asset and expense categories should be utilized. Decision models used by management are becoming more explicit and should be availed of for this purpose. Studies that quantify the benefits of advertising and of research expenditures are becoming more prevalent, and where applicable should be used.[1]

To date, few formal steps have been taken toward allocating advertising costs to the benefits generated by such costs.

Allocation of advertising costs is not a revolutionary concept. In 1911 Elijah Watts Sells was advocating that advertising expenditures be amortized over their productive lives:

> Generally speaking, such advertising as may be done for the purpose of bringing some new business or branch of business, some new or improved article or articles to the attention of the public, which has a

---

[1] *A Statement of Basic Accounting Theory* (American Accounting Association, 1966), p. 35.

direct effect in creating or measurably increasing the good will of a business undertaking, may be considered as an investment in that there has been an appreciable increase in the amount of capital employed....[2]

In earlier years the control of production costs was essential, and the management accountant devoted much effort to the proper matching of production costs to the revenues produced. Production costs were so important that the past half-century of cost accounting development has been devoted primarily to methods of allocating the costs of producing the finished product. Now marketing costs such as advertising and new-product development are taking a greater bite out of the total sales dollar. Management accountants should exert increased effort to allocate marketing costs properly to correspond to the revenues resulting from such costs.

The proper allocation of advertising and new-product development costs is one part of an effective managment information system for new-product decision makers. When management knows what return it receives and can relate that performance to prior investments, then more effective management will be possible. The costs of developing and selling a new product are certainly as important as the costs of manufacturing. The field of allocation of production costs has been exploited previously. The area of marketing costs, particularly those relating to a new product, is still a frontier in accounting.

Accounting Use of Life Cycle Models

Some of the respondents in our study indicated that their companies already were using product life cycle models to develop budget figures, which probably comes as a surprise to most accountants. Consequently, further education in the use of life cycle models should be a topic of concern to management accountants who do not use such models at present.

Cost allocation is another area in which life cycle models could be used beneficially for accounting purposes. If the new-product decision maker could provide the accountants with a probable life cycle for each new product, then the accountants could allocate the development costs and base ROI statistics on that model. As mentioned in Chapter 2, life cycle models already are being used for

---

[2]Elijah W. Sells, "Should Advertising Expenditures Be Charged as an Investment or as an Expense?" *Journal of Accountancy* (September 1911), p. 346.

pricing and promotional purposes. Thus, it seems reasonable that accountants could use the same models to prepare budgets and the subsequent budget reports. Though some product life cycles probably can never be predicted accurately, many types of products do lend themselves to this method of analysis. The time spent on this kind of foresight adds a more rational approach to the budgeting and cost allocation processes. Unfortunately, accountants are not fully aware of the technical aspects of product life cycle models so are not yet capable of using such models for allocation and budgeting purposes.

The Need for More Analysis by Accountants

Although some of the accountants in this study provided tools such as sensitivity and risk analysis, they were far from a majority. Because marketing decision makers typically do not have a strong accounting background, it is even more important for accountants to analyze the data provided.

Accountants probably also need to do more analysis in the area of pricing alternatives. ROI statistics often are based on sophisticated estimates of production costs, but they also are based on prices established by "gut feeling." The respondents in this study indicated that analyses often are not conducted to determine optimum pricing strategies. Also, prices are not really based on costs. Instead, the price is predetermined in some manner, and then costs are examined to see if the product can be marketed profitably. Someone—perhaps the accountants—should be concerned with price elasticity and the effect alternative prices might have on the abandonment rate for new products.

Areas for Future Study

We already have mentioned some areas for future study. Another study similar to this one perhaps should be conducted—but using companies within a single industry. Our results indicate that those companies in the same industry often are quite similar in their new-product decision processes. Even nationality does not make too much difference, as indicated by the two sporting goods manufacturers.

Another idea for further study would be to compare successful companies with unsuccessful companies. Our study could not differentiate between successful and unsuccessful. All the managers in this study indicated that they were quite successful, and there is nothing to contradict those statements.

Limitations

Caution should be used in generalizing results beyond the companies included in the study because the study was based on a limited, nonrandom sample. However, their experiences can serve as a guide for other companies. The companies selected were those which were quite large and in which the new-product decision process was ongoing and organized. Companies such as these were presumed to have given greater managerial attention to the decision process, thus making them a better source for learning the intricacies of what managers consider before introducing a new product.

We also did not attempt to consider all additional relationships between the new-product decision process and other types of managerial decisions. New-product decisions are not made in a vacuum. For example, the pricing decision (which was examined in an earlier study sponsored by NAA and SMAC) is actually a part of the new-product decision, yet we did not delve deeply into the roots of the pricing decision as a part of this study. Similarly, one can argue that the product abandonment decision is at least somewhat related to the new-product decision. Again, however, the product abandonment decision is being examined in another study. In reality, the new-product decision probably should be examined in the context of a company's total decision-making process, but such a complete study would not be practical. Thus, examining a single decision process in a vacuum represents a limitation of this study—but a necessary one. Despite these limitations, this study should help the reader to understand the new-product decision process.

Conclusions

We examined the new-product decision process at 17 companies in the United States and Canada. The companies included in our survey were rather large and quite successful, and all emphasized the importance of new products to the company's future success. Apparently there was no problem with a lack of managerial support at any company, and new-product decision makers were given a free hand with few budget constraints.

Canadian companies were not too different from those in the United States. The Canadians were more imitative than their southern neighbors and were more apt to use a committee system to evaluate new-product decisions. Canadians also were less apt to use test markets to obtain information about a new-product's chances for success. This failure to use test markets, however, probably is because the product usually imitated a product already successful in the United States. Consequently, market data from the United States were extrapolated to the Canadian market.

We uncovered a variety of decision processes in this study. Unfortunately, we could not determine whether any are more successful than others. Because all the processes seemed successful, there was no way to measure effectiveness. Also, there was no way to evaluate the failure rates in the different industries, especially as many companies did not know their failure rates. Perhaps if accountants were to develop some standardized reporting system for new-product decision makers, then it might be possible to evaluate the decision process more effectively.

Heretofore, accountants have taken the easy road with respect to accounting for the costs of new-product development. Pragmatism cannot be the only factor in making a journal entry. The area of providing accounting information for new-product decision makers is still a frontier in accounting, and we hope this study has taken one small step into that frontier.

Selected Bibliography

Abernathy, W. J. and N. Baloff. "Concepts, Theory, and Technique: A Methodology for Planning New Product Start-Ups." *Decision Sciences,* 4 (1973): 1-21.

Albala, Americo. "A Model for New Product Planning." *Long Range Planning,* December 1977, pp. 62-69.

——————. "Financial Planning for New Products." *Long Range Planning,* August 1977, pp. 61-69.

Assmus, Gert. "NEWPROD: The Design and Implementation of a New Product Model." *Journal of Marketing,* January 1975, pp. 16-23.

"Avoiding New Product Failure." *The Accountant,* 19 May 1977, p. 574.

Ayal, Igal. "Simple Models for Monitoring New Product Performance." *Decision Sciences,* 6 (1975): 221-236.

Beardsley, George. "A Note on the Accuracy of Industrial Forecasts of the Profitability of New Products and Processes." *Journal of Business,* 51 (1978): 127-135.

Brown, Merrill. "Marketing Expert Foresees Era of Superbrands." *Clarion-Ledger* (Jackson, Miss.), December 17, 1982, p. D-1.

Clifford, Donald K., Jr. "Leverage in the Product Life Cycle." *Dun's Review,* May 1965, pp. 62-64.

"Companies Which Develop Most New Products Have Good Growth." *Iron Age,* 6 September 1976, p. 19.

Cooper, Robert G. and Blair Little. "Determinants of Market Research Expenditures for New Industrial Products." *Industrial Marketing Management,* 6 (1977): 102-112.

Crawford, C. Merle. "Marketing Research and the New Product Failure Rate." *Journal of Marketing,* April 1977, pp. 51-61.

Dean, Joel. "Pricing Policies for New Products." *Harvard Business Review,* November-December 1976, pp. 141-153.

Dillon, William R., Roger Calantone and Parker Worthing. "The New-Product Problem: An Approach for Investigating Product Failures." *Management Science,* 25 (December 1979): 1184-1195.

Dusenbury, Warren. "CPM for New Product Introductions." *Harvard Business Review,* July-August 1967, pp. 124-139.

Eggleston, David. "New Product Development." *Management Controls,* September 1973, pp. 214-215.

Evans, Richard H. "Assessing Introduction Factors for a New Industrial Product." *Industrial Marketing Management,* 7 (1978): 128-132.

Gerlach, John T., and Charles Anthony Wainwright. *Successful Management of New Products.* New York: Hastings House, 1968.

Gisser, Philip. "New Products Are a Gamble, but the Risk Can Be Reduced." *Industrial Marketing,* May 1973, pp. 28-32.

Gordon, Lawrence A., Danny Miller and Henry Mintzberg. *Normative Models in Managerial Decision Making.* New York: National Association of Accountants, 1975.

Heller, Roger M. and Thomas P. Hustad. "Problems in Predicting New Product Growth for Consumer Durables." *Management Science,* 26 (October 1973): 1007-1020.

Holmes, John H. "Profitable Product Positioning." *Business Topics,* 21 (Spring 1973): 27-32.

Hopkins, David S. *New Product Winners and Losers.* New York: The Conference Board, 1980.

_____. *Options in New Product Organization.* New York: The Conference Board, 1974.

Howell, Sydney D. "Learning Curves for New Products." *Industrial Marketing Management,* 9 (1980): 97-99.

Imbro, Andrew. "New Products and Their Related Costs." *Management Accounting,* August 1971, pp. 43-44.

Information for Marketing Management. New York: National Association of Accountants, 1971.

Ingrassia, Paul. "P & G's Rivals Often Show Up at Fred's Place." *Wall Street Journal,* November 1, 1982, pp. 1 ff.

Lang, John B. *Finding a New Product for Your Company.* Washington, D.C.: U.S. Small Business Administration, 1981.

Larson, Gustav E. *Developing and Selling New Products.* Washington D.C.: U.S. Government Printing Office, 1949.

Levitt, Theodore. "Exploit the Product Life Cycle." *Harvard Business Review,* November-December 1965, p. 81.

Linehan, Thomas A. "Communications Boosts Chance of New Product Acceptance." *Industrial Marketing,* September 1977, pp. 46-52.

148

Lindberg, Bertil C. "International Comparison of Growth in Demand for a New Durable Consumer Product." *Journal of Marketing Research,* August 1982, pp. 364-371.

MacKensie, George F. "MacKensie: On Marketing's 'Missing Link'—the Product Life Cycle Concept." *Industrial Marketing,* April 1971, pp. 42-43.

Mansfield, Edwin and John Rappaport. "The Costs of Industrial Product Innovations." *Management Science,* 21 (August 1975): 1380-1386.

McGuire, E. Patrick. *Generating New Product Ideas.* New York: The Conference Board, Inc., 1972.

Merrifield, D. Bruce. "How to Select Successful R & D Projects." *Management Review,* December 1978, pp. 25-37.

Midgley, David F. *Innovation and New Product Marketing.* New York: John Wiley & Sons, 1977.

Moran, William T. "Why New Products Fail." *Journal of Advertising Research,* 13 (April 1973): 5-13.

New, D. E., and J. L. Schlacter. "Abandon Bad R & D Projects with Earlier Marketing Appraisals." *Industrial Marketing Management,* 8 (1979): 274-280.

Nylen, David W. "New-Product Failures: Not Just a Marketing Problem." *Business,* 29 (September-October 1979): 2-7.

Parsons, Leonard J. "An Econometric Analysis of Advertising, Retail Availability, and Sales of a New Brand." *Management Science,* 20 (February 1974): 938-947.

Paschkes, Michael. "How to Guarantee New Product Failures." *Sales and Marketing Management,* 12 July 1976, pp. 40-42.

Rothberg, Robert R. "Playing It Safe in New Product Decisions." *S.A.M. Advanced Management Journal,* Autumn 1975, pp. 11-19.

Sands, Saul. "Can Business Afford the Luxury of Test Marketing?" *University of Michigan Business Review,* March 1978, pp. 19-24.

Scanlon, Sally. "Zeroing in on Profits." *Sales and Marketing Management,* March 1978, pp. 61-76.

Smallwood, John E. "The Product Life Cycle: A Key to Strategic Marketing Planning." *MSU Business Topics,* Winter 1973, pp. 31-37.

Spencer, Edson W. "The Marketing Man as Entrepreneur: A Look at His Role in Building Profits." *Industrial Marketing,* June 1976, pp. 112-116.

Stauff, James A. R. *How to Plan and Develop New Products That Sell.* Chicago: Dartnell Press, 1974.

Stumpe, Warren R. "Who Pays for New Product Development?" *Research Management,* September 1978, pp. 17-19.

Tauber, Edward M. "Forecasting Sales Prior to Test Market." *Journal of Marketing,* January 1977, pp. 80-84.

Udell, Gerald C. *New Product Development.* Washington, D.C.: U. S. Small Business Administration.

Urban, Glen. "SPRINTER Mod III: A Model for the Analysis of New Frequently Purchased Consumer Products." *Operations Research,* September-October 1970, pp. 805-853.

Urban, Glen C., and John R. Hauser. *Design and Marketing of New Products.* Englewood Cliffs, N.J.: Prentice-Hall, Inc., 1980.

Von Hipple, Eric. "Get New Products from Customers." *Harvard Business Review,* March-April 1982, pp. 117-122.